MEDICAL DEVICE MARKETING

MEDICAL DEVICE MARKETING:

*Strategies, Gameplans &
Resources for Successful
Product Management*

TERRI WELLS

Outskirts Press, Inc.
Denver, Colorado

The opinions expressed in this manuscript are solely the opinions of the author and do not represent the opinions or thoughts of the publisher. The author has represented and warranted full ownership and/or legal right to publish all the materials in this book.

Medical Device Marketing:
Strategies, Gameplans & Resources for Successful Product Management
All Rights Reserved.
Copyright © 2010 Terri Wells
v3.0

This book may not be reproduced, transmitted, or stored in whole or in part by any means, including graphic, electronic, or mechanic, without the express written consent of the publisher except in the case of brief quotations embodied in critical articles and reviews.

Outskirts Press, Inc.
http://www.outskirtspress.com

ISBN: 978-1-4327-5072-5

Library of Congress Control Number: 2010926618

Outskirts Press and the "OP" logo are trademarks belonging to Outskirts Press, Inc.

PRINTED IN THE UNITED STATES OF AMERICA

Contents

Author's Note 1
Introduction 3

Chapter 1 What is so Different About Medical Device Marketing? 5
    Who is the customer? 5
    Decision-making now – what does it look like today? 7
    The buyer…or follow the money 8
    Fundamentals of reimbursement and healthcare economics 11
    The letter of the law 17
    Ethics and responsibility 19

Chapter 2 Building a Business Plan (and Controlling Your Destiny) 21
    Market research 21
    Assessing opportunity 25
    Financial analysis 26
    Project scope 28
    The stage gate process 29

Chapter 3 Product Development: Managing Issues and Meeting Deadlines .. 39
    Project definition… 39
    Financial targets 40
    Physician input 41
    FDA approval and reimbursement…behind the scenes 43
    Managing issues/ meeting deadlines 48
    Appendix 49

Chapter 4 Getting Product Launches Right 53
    Forecasting: putting the horse in front of the cart 53
    Pricing 60

                Product and sales support 66
                Appendix 75

Chapter 5 Managing an Existing Product Line, Successfully 85
                Connecting to the sales team 85
                New is always better…is it not?... 90
                Analyzing an existing product line 91
                To update or not?.. 92
                Appendix 96

Chapter 6 Product Phase-Out -- the Toughest Job............................... 101
                Phase-out checklist 101
                Assessing lifecycle, customers, and competition..................... 103
                Financials - balancing sales, profit, and inventory................. 110
                Marketing/ pricing analysis... 113
                Distribution decisions and timing.. 113
                Promotion possibilities... 114
                Communication externally – to the field and to the customers 115

Chapter 7 What Does it Take to be a Product Manager in Medical Device?. 121
                The product manager role.. 121
                Sales and marketing – working together 129
                Critical skill sets... 130
                Appendix 133

Chapter 8 Tips and Tricks to Make Life Easier, Plus Some Invaluable
                Resources 143
                Pesky marketing fundamentals 143
                What does 'upstream' versus 'downstream' mean in
                marketing? 147
                Resources for gathering data, and generally helpful info 150

Conclusion 157

Author's Note

I started my career in the medical device field over twenty years ago. In that time I have noticed that there simply are not many resources available for marketing professionals in this field. While the industry is growing and constantly expanding, it is not nearly as large as either the consumer or pharmaceutical business, and I assume that this is much of the reason for a lack of material.

Over the last several years, I have witnessed many examples of good candidates who were placed in medical device marketing positions with no training and no real reference guides for support. Then, they were essentially challenged to sink or swim on their own. I have looked numerous times to find something to assist these individuals but have been unsuccessful in finding any relevant materials. My reason for writing this book is to try and address this situation. It is my hope is that this can help those new to the industry as well as give a few ideas to those whom have been in it a while.

I have been lucky over the years to have been on several great teams inside some good organizations. As with everything, there have been both difficult and straightforward situations to work though, and the individuals with whom I have worked have been professional, driven and good at what they do. I have learned much from many of them and wish I had the space to thank them all individually. It will have to suffice to say that I truly appreciate all of my coworkers in marketing, the sales and engineering teams with which I have worked, the managers who have been instrumental in my development and career path, and, of course, all of the surgeons who make this industry possible.

Most everything contained in this book is based on my thoughts and opinions about best practices after learning, observing, and doing virtually every aspect of medical device marketing. While there are methods and ideas that I do not have any experience with – different companies approach problems differently and new ideas spring from consulting companies every day – the fundamental principles of marketing and business practice still apply. Thus, I routinely hear of new concepts from industry and field-based sources that may or may not be better than the ones contained in the book; however, I know that the basic theories and rules will still hold true.

One other point that needs to be addressed is the ever-present legal and regulatory obligations on the medical device industry. All device promotion is subject to the codes, laws, and rulings within the local market (and sometimes to that of the parent organization as well.) Regulatory and legal pathways change quickly and frequently, and I want to carefully point out that my expertise is in marketing. I am not an attorney, and I do not claim that this book can be used as a guide to the legal or regulatory maze of the medical device industry. While I have provided some notes to alert a product manager of legal and regulatory potential concerns, I want to clearly state that nothing contained in this book should be used or relied upon to make a legal or regulatory decision.

On a personal note, this book would not have made it this far without the strong support of my family. My husband, David, helped by both handling a tremendous amount of parenting responsibilities and sidelined as counselor/coach as well. Additionally, my children, Rachel and Megan, were supportive and patient as my writing time sometimes cut into some family activities.

Finally, I would also like to thank two other people, David Yawn and Greg Kretovic. David did a great job editing this book. He handled that task with speed and efficiency and truly helped transform my first draft into a more polished work. Greg used his outstanding graphic design skills to take all of my charts and graphs from a variety of different programs and quickly create a single, consistent format that easily works throughout the book.

Thanks to many others who provided advice and feedback, and to those who offered encouragement to keep going along the way. Much appreciation and gratitude is sent from me to you.

Introduction

Consumer marketing has the 4Ps – product, price, promotion, and place – sometimes joined in more recent times by packaging and positioning. While this sounds good, trying to apply principles of classical marketing theory to medical device marketing is like the typical case of trying to place a square peg into a round hole, in other words, close but not quite.

To cope, most device industry product managers select those pieces of marketing philosophy that make the most sense and follow those principles loosely, hoping for the best. The ones who stay in device marketing for a while end up developing their own systems, tricks, and rules of thumb that complement, supplement, or replace what was originally learned in a marketing course.

Medical device product managers come from a variety of backgrounds and with a range of experience levels. Because of the high technical demands of the job, a greater percentage come with engineering training than in the marketing department of most industries. However, device product managers can also come from the sales force, a clinical background in the operating room, the nursing or physical therapy ranks.

Another conduit into device marketing is through other functions within the medical device company itself. While any function can theoretically be a stepping stone (for instance, moving from an accounting/finance position that worked closely with the sales and marketing teams into a full-time marketing role), the most common pathways are through sister departments such as business development, market research, sales training, or marketing communications. The common theme to all these routes, however, is that the typical path into device marketing requires development of one or more of the following: specific device-related knowledge, clinical background, or sales and surgeon interaction.

The purpose of this book is to shine a light on medical device marketing, the theory and the practice, along with some real-life cases and practical examples. Ideas, references, and illustrations are all intended to illuminate what a successful device product manager does and to stimulate thoughts on how one might handle a specific situation or event. Additionally, a greater goal is to increase the overall competency within the field of device marketing and hopefully, even inspire conversations about aspects of device marketing that should be improved.

The world of medical devices is changing rapidly, shifting faster today than ever before. Not only are these swift changes a result of the information age and global marketplace that we all live in, but also due to the worldwide economic pressures that drive scrutiny of every dollar spent on healthcare. The focus of medical device marketing professionals must be to hear and understand these pressures and to work within the framework of their organizations to respond with true innovation. Window-dressing product changes that are called 'innovation', with insubstantial benefits and higher prices are quickly losing ground *and just as importantly*, these types of 'marketing' plans weaken the ability to demonstrate and justify truly effective innovation.

Medical device marketing as a whole influences the perception of patients, physicians, providers, and payers in determining the true value of devices -- now and in the future. The product manager role stretches in both directions – strategy based on environment and company awareness and tactics based on everyday execution and last-minute responses. It is an opportunity to influence and to interact, to become a valuable component of a high-level discussion and assist the sales team. It involves really being an integral part of the company which makes medical device marketing in general and the product manager role specifically so compelling.

CHAPTER 1

What is so Different About Medical Device Marketing?

Marketing is not the same in every industry. Two of the better known marketing arenas are in pharmaceuticals and consumer products (clothing, food, etc.) While both of these areas have unique challenges and require specialized expertise, the skill set and job description of a marketer in medical devices is quite different than either of these. This book will go through the specific capabilities, experience, and some tips on how to be excellent in medical device marketing. Whether you are already in medical device marketing or you want to break into the field, this book will help you understand what it takes to do the job…and to do it right.

Who is the customer?

In a typical marketing class, you talk about B2B or B2C and strategies to reach the decision-makers. In medical device marketing, defining the customer is an exercise all in itself. As the marketing 'brains' of the operation, you need to carefully consider this question to have a coherent target in developing a marketing message and campaign for your product(s) – if you simply "do" and don't stop to think , you leave it up to the sales team 'brawn' to do the work for you. Therefore, stop to consider who the decision-maker is first.

To help with this process, here are some possible customers for your consideration:
1. The health care provider (or HCP) – Often this is a surgeon in medical devices, but not necessarily. The HCP is generally the focus customer because he/she makes the final call on what medical device to use in the O.R. If it is the surgeon who is targeted, then he/she has responsibility for patient outcome and typically makes O.R. device decisions; however,

the surgeon's decision-making powers are not absolute.

2. The sales representative – This is sometimes an odd choice in most industries but one that makes sense in medical devices. The sales representative is the conduit to the surgeon and has the relationships to navigate the hospital as well. It is not uncommon for the surgeon to remain loyal to the sales representative if he or she changes companies. Why? This is because the sales representative provides an invaluable service. On a routine basis, the representative ensures the surgeon has all the implants and instruments for the case and handles in-servicing with the O.R staff before the surgery. A top-notch, experienced representative also acts in the capacity of a consultant/advisor in the event that a surgery does not go as planned. This relationship transcends mere service and its value to the surgeon is tremendous. Thus, there is an argument for making the sales representative a major focus in developing marketing materials and related messages.

3. The patient – Ultimately it is the patient who receives the implant, who the surgeon is focused on, and for whom the product is developed. As more patients (or their caretakers) gather information on the internet, their participation in the decision-making process is far more meaningful than in the past. Historically, patients relied on their surgeons to simply implant the "best" device for them. However, as new technology becomes available, there is an emerging segment of activist patients who gather information and demand the right to be an active participant in determining what implant is used. Some surgeons actively encourage this -- others are less open to these conversations. Regardless, the patient is now a candidate for direct-to-consumer messaging/ marketing campaign, particularly if presented and managed in the form of patient education.

4. The hospital – Very few marketing people or companies focus on the hospital as a major customer, but increasingly the hospital plays a significant role in determining what implant is used, when it can be used, and what profile patient it can be used on. Many hospitals have limited the surgeon's choices by reducing the number of vendors who are allowed in the hospital, and in some cases, the choices have been severely cut back. The difficulty with targeting the hospital as the customer is figuring out *who* exactly to target: the executives, the purchaser/buyers, the OR supervisor, etc. However, more and

more, these groups should at least be considered while developing the marketing plan and message for the sales representative to use in influencing the sales cycle.

Decision-making now – what does it look like today?

With all these influences over the purchase decision, it is helpful to have an understanding of how the decision-making process works for the particular product (or product category) for your campaign development. It is likely that there will be significant regional variation as well as differences among teaching centers, suburban hospitals, and rural hospitals. However, a baseline grasp helps in constructing a draft message, campaign plan, and sales funnel outline that can then be evaluated and refined.

For comparison sake, here are two closely related device markets – and the rough estimates in who holds the decision-making power for each:

	Hip & Knee	Spine
Surgeon	55-65%	75-80%
Patient	5-10%	0-5%
Hospital Buying Group/ Purchasing Committee	20-40%	15-25%
Hospital O.R. Supervisor	0-5%	0-2%

NOTE: The sales representative is generally not considered directly as part of this equation, although he/she certainly influences the surgeon and hospital staff's understanding of the product and what is appropriate or reasonable.

SECOND NOTE: In interpreting these percentages and applying them to other areas within medical device applications, it is worth noting that the spine device market is considered 'younger' and more volatile than the hip and knee device market. In general, there is not as much consensus on indications and more variability in types and styles of devices used based on surgeon preference for spine surgery. Not only have spine devices been used and developed for fewer years than hip and knee, but also there are a number of questions and controversies in the arena that have yet to be answered by scientific studies on the biomechanics of the normal, diseased, and corrected spines. Based on the changes seen in the hip/knee market as it grew, and as the spine device arena continues to mature, the decision-making power may also shift away from surgeons and toward hospitals and patients over time.

With the changes to the healthcare system under discussion and sensitivity to delivering real value at minimal cost, the shift in decision-making power is likely to trend toward the hospital, with the Purchasing Committees and the Buyers at the helm. However, as long as medical malpractice focuses on the surgeon, they will have a "say" in what is used. If the hospitals and surgeons can agree on how to appropriately assess cost and value, then decision-making may become less adversarial and more cooperative. A different relationship paradigm between hospitals and surgeons will likely result in a significant shift in how decisions are made as well.

The buyer...or follow the money

Once the surgeon has decided to use the product and the hospital allows it in the facility, who actually pays for it? Initially, the hospital pays the device company for the implant and any disposables used during surgery. Thus, the easy and direct answer for 'who is the buyer' is the hospital, and the great majority of the time that's all there is to it...but there is a significant minority that you need to know about.

AN ALTERNATIVE

In today's world of high-cost technology and cost-squeezing insurance, it doesn't always work that the hospital is the buyer. There are companies such as Access Mediquip that will act as intermediaries between the hospital, the insurance company, the patient, and the device company to pay for the implant. In these cases, the intermediary firm (i.e. Access Mediquip, www.accessmediquip.com) negotiates ahead of time with the hospital to pay for the implant, and in return, accept the reimbursement due from the insurance company for the prosthesis/implant. The hospital only gets reimbursed for the rest of the procedure – OR room time, anesthesia, OR supplies, and any other bundled charges for soft goods, etc.

The intermediary company will contact the insurer ahead of time just as the hospital would to ensure that the procedure is pre-approved and will also make certain that the insurance company is aware of the split in fees. Any difficulty in collecting from the insurance company is a risk borne by the intermediary. If charges are not allowed or are above usual and customary rates, then the intermediary firm must attempt to collect from the patient just as the hospital would. Thus, the surgeon is typically aware of the arrangement also because of the possibility of patient contact. The device company receives payment from the intermediary firm, not from the hospital, and often at lower discount rate/ higher prices than they would get directly from the hospital.

While these arrangements comprise less than 20% of all device surgeries and are typically reserved only for higher-end, more costly technology, it is a payment mechanism worth being aware of, and perhaps proactively advocating if it allows a patient to receive needed technology that they otherwise wouldn't be able to receive

The conundrum

This brings us to the conundrum of device buying – the purchaser is most often removed from the decision-maker, with an uneasy alliance at best. Thus, the surgeon wants what is best for the patient, easiest, fastest and most reliable in the O.R., and supported by a known and respected sales rep. He or she is also the person held accountable for patient outcomes and is held liable under medical malpractice laws. The hospital/purchaser wants reasonable and adequate care and may not see the easiest, fastest or most reliable benefits as worth additional dollars. Thus starts the arguments between *adequate* care/technology and *best-in-class/state-of-the-art* care and technology.

The hospital has an annual budget to meet – with devices as one component of a thousand lines of expenses. If new technology (*often read: higher prices*) come into the picture or a surgeon suddenly changes the practice mix to the extent that the average price per procedure increases substantially, then the budget is out of whack. Then it becomes a shell game of robbing Peter to pay Paul...with Peter usually fully aware of the game and resisting with all his might. These politics and the need to run a business, as well as provide ethical quality care, is a tightrope balancing act that puts a strain on an already difficult love/hate triangle between hospital, surgeon, and the device companies.

Insurance company puzzle piece

The insurance company also has a piece of the puzzle that is often not well understood, and thus usually ignored. However, although it is complex, it can make a big difference in approaching a market. Each insurance company negotiates with each hospital they do business with – a separate contract that covers how they will calculate payments, what is bundled inside and how (or if) new technology is considered. (Incidentally, the insurance company also negotiates individually with each surgeon on payments, although many surgeons allow the hospital to negotiate on their behalf. This is not a commentary on the practice, just a side note.)

Thus, there is absolutely NO WAY to know how much a hospital is getting paid for a procedure or implant…or even exactly how it is being calculated… *unless they tell you.* Even if they tell you, beware of the fine print! An insurance company's contract with a hospital is about as complex as the tax code – with as many individual variations. It is virtually impossible to decipher from the outside looking in. Just as each medical device company has unique pricing contracts with each hospital (or purchasing group), the hospital will have a unique and individual contract with each insurance company.

However, there are a few main ways that insurance companies reimburse hospitals for device procedures (and this is only about device procedures):

Payment type	Brief description
DRG	Procedure bundling, generally follows Medicare rates although each hospital will negotiate specific rates based on their length of stay, cost, patient mix, etc.
DRG w/ carve-out	Similar to above but with a carve-out for the implant. The implant is then reimbursed separately, per contract. Some hospitals will use this to provide for mix shifts and new technology.
Cost plus	Hospital is reimbursed based on actual cost plus some % above (plus-up). Not often seen, but still exists in rare/ special cases.
Per diem	Reimbursement based on patient stay, often with amount high at beginning of stay and reducing dramatically each day.
Case rate	Type of surgery determines amount of reimbursement. Procedures are usually fairly well-defined and specific.
Fee-for-service	Each part of the procedure, from surgeon fees to patient charge items to lab tests, are charged and reimbursed separately based on a negotiated rate for each line item.
Discounted fee-for-service	Similar to above, but with some discount a cap applied per line item.
Technology carve-outs/ upcharges	Specific carve-outs or upcharges that can be applied to virtually any of the payments above based on technology or sicker patient or some other outlier. However, these have to be pre-negotiated and part of the contract ahead of time.

For each DRG, CMS (Medicare) publishes data regarding payment that gives a general idea of how much is reimbursed. However, the hospital-specific amount is adjusted based on the case/mix index each year that accounts for how sick their patients are. Other factors are multiplied, such as whether the account is a teaching hospital or a trauma center or even classified as rural. All these items can dramatically impact the base DRG value, and also factors into when the hospital is negotiating with private insurers.

One website to check if you want to get more hospital-specific information is www.ahd.com. Data is available online for free; however with a subscription, you can find very detailed financial information about a hospital. This particularly helps with DRG data. Subscriptions run at $395 per year. However, even with that data, there is still no way to fully know exactly what a hospital is being reimbursed per procedures, especially across a range of private, commercial insurers.

Fundamentals of reimbursement and healthcare economics

Now that the topic of reimbursement has been brought up, it is worth delving into deeper. Historically, this has not been a topic that medical device product managers have understood or been well versed in, and generally, they had not needed to be. However, as healthcare economics become a larger issue, globalization becomes more than just a nice word and innovation pushes the boundaries of the device world, thus reimbursement has become a much greater issue. Product managers need to understand enough about reimbursement to assess regulatory, profitability, and risk, plus be able to carry on intelligent conversations with consultants, surgeons, and hospital executives about the fundamentals of the medical device business in general and their products in particular.

In essence, this section is intended to be a crash course in the basics of terminology, reimbursement, and health economic basics useful in considering and constructing a marketing plan. If reimbursement is truly an issue and in-depth analysis is needed, you will definitely want to engage specific expertise for guidance.

TERMS TO BE FAMILIAR WITH

The following terms will come up over and over in any discussion involving reimbursement. Knowing these acronyms and what they really mean can help you in conversation – plus help establish your creditability that you in fact know what you're talking about.

◂ MEDICAL DEVICE MARKETING

Acronym	Meaning	Explanation/ Comments
ICD-9	International Classification of Diseases - 9th revision	Will sometimes see ICD-10, which indicates the 10th revision. Outside U.S. already uses and U.S. moves to it in 2013. Example - 715.0 - Osteoarthritis as DJD.
DRG	Diagnostic Related Group - organizes ICD-9 codes into 'groups'	This is how CMS (Medicare/ Medicaid) pays for procedures. The DRG Relative Weight x the Hospital Base Rate = Hospital Payment for the procedure. The payment covers ALL OR expenses, post-op, and even any complications that occur for up to 90 days after
CPT	Current Procedural Terminology - describes service & procedures	A 5 digit number that is used by the physician to describe service or procedure. CPT codes are assigned by the AMA with review/ help from the Specialty Societies and determine the RVU for each item. This determines how much the physician is paid - but each time a new code is created or an RVU goes up, something else goes down! Very political.
RVU	Relative Value Unit - the multiplier that is used to calculate surgeon payment	Number split into 3 parts to reflect the providers' work/ time/ training required, malpractice expense, practice expense. Each CPT has an RVU.
GPCI	Geographic Practice Cost Index	Another multiplier that accounts for the economic variation per region.
HCPCs	Health Care Procedure Coding System	Covers other services, products, and supplies not found in CPT codes. Example - E series codes covers all Durable Medical Equipment & J series covers all Drug Codes (other than oral).

HOW IT WORKS TOGETHER...

ICD-9 codes are the backbone of BOTH hospital and surgeon coding – it is used to describe why the patient was treated and what was done. In the patient record, the ICD-9 codes link the diagnoses, procedures, and co-morbidities. All DRG and CPT codes must link to the ICD-9 in order for reimbursement payments to be processed.

It is worth noting that the ICD-9 and CPT codes are standardized across all private insurance companies and CMS. Thus, while the payment and approvals vary widely, the codes always stand for the same things and link together the same way.

Another code example:

- 812.22 is a diagnosis code for fracture of the humerus.
- 733.9 is the code that describes a patient with Osteoporosis as a co-morbidity.
- The hip resurfacing procedure was granted a new code in late 2006; for resurfacing of the head and acetabulum the code is 00.85.

DRGs are used to group like ICD-9 codes/procedures together and then CMS/ Medicare bases payment on the DRG group. The DRG 'relative

WHAT IS SO DIFFERENT ABOUT MEDICAL DEVICE MARKETING?

weight' is multiplied by the Hospital Base Payment to get the hospital-specific reimbursement. The DRG relative weight is based on a review by CMS of several factors: severity of the illness, probable outcome, treatment difficulty/ patient management issues, need for immediate intervention (versus elective), resource intensity. The hospital base payment is calculated based on the location (rural, suburban, urban, teaching, etc.) and case/mix index (how sick on average their patients are). However, commercial insurance companies will use the overall DRG relative weight/ payment structure also to develop baseline calculations. Typically, the commercial rates are higher by 1.2-2x CMS, but not always.

Remember that CPT codes are the basis for how physicians get paid because they are where the service or procedure RVU (relative value unit) is assigned. This is very critical when looking at reimbursement because if the physician/surgeon doesn't get paid for doing a procedure, then the likelihood of a success goes way down. So that you are more comfortable with the concept and building blocks of the RVU, here's how it works:

There are three parts to an RVU.

 Physician Work RVU - Value of physician work, time training, expertise, etc.

 Practice Expense RVU - Value of expenses incurred maintaining practice (rent, staff, utilities, supplies, etc.)

 Malpractice Expense RVU - Value of expense associated with malpractice insurance/risk.

These three components, when added together create the total RVU.

Note: There is a GPCI factor for each RVU segment that is applied also.

Example: 27130 - Total hip replacement

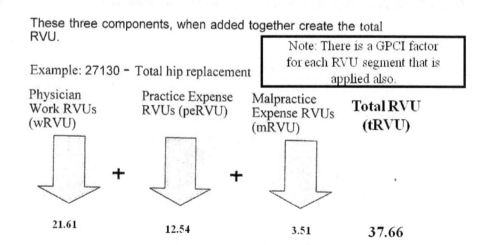

◄ MEDICAL DEVICE MARKETING

Once the RVU has been determined, the CMS sets the conversion factor and updates it on a yearly basis. For 2009, the conversion factor for surgical services was $37.8975. Thus, for Total Hip Replacement code 27130, the surgeon was paid $37.8975 * 37.66 (the tRVU) for a total of $1,427.23.

BIG PICTURE — WHO PAYS FOR WHAT?

Once codes are established and the procedure (or service) has the proper information, then what? It often depends on what the target patient population is as to who the final payer really is. Thus, if a large percentage of the patient population is over 65 or if it helps a specific population of the disabled, then CMS is likely the main payer. If a broader spectrum of patients is likely, or if younger patients are the norm, then private insurance comes heavily into play.

This does NOT mean, however, that CMS is not important — private insurers look to CMS to establish codes and often to establish approximate reimbursement relative values as well. Additionally, CMS can issue a no-coverage or lack-of-equivalence ruling that significantly impairs the ability to obtain reimbursement from the private payer marketplace.

On an overall view of the U.S., the graph below gives a perspective on how healthcare is paid. Please note that this does not discuss international markets where socialized medicine is often the norm. However, even in many of these markets, a public/private pay system often exists where patients either opt out of the public-pay system or supplement it with privately-held insurance.

U.S. Healthcare Payment — Who Pays?

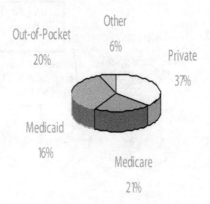

Source: 1998 Data. HCFA, Office of the Actuary, National Health Statistics Group. January, 2000.

In the U.S., a bit more than 1/3 of all healthcare bills are ultimately footed by CMS – Medicare for the elderly and Medicaid for children and those otherwise incapacitated. Roughly 2/3 of healthcare are private pay or self-pay. Indigent (unpaid) care is not accounted for in this model.

It is worth noting that there are roughly 4,500 private payers. The top 5 nationally known insurers are United, Cigna, Aetna, the Blues, and Humana. However, there are also several very strong regional private insurers – Kaiser, Harvard, Pilgrim UPMC, to name a few. In order to successfully gain coverage with private insurers, a game plan on how to approach, who to approach, and in what order is definitely needed.

The game plan

There really is not 'a' game plan...but there are some fundamental blocking and tackling strategies and tactics that anyone building a game plan needs to know. The first of these is building a case for CMS, not just for FDA. While the FDA determines safety and efficacy of a device, CMS is charged with assessing whether it is reasonable and medically necessary (for a Medicare population). Thus, they look for data showing improved health outcomes for Medicare beneficiaries *over* existing treatments/ technologies. It is VERY important to notice that *efficacy* (does it work) is the domain of the FDA and *effectiveness* (does it work better) is the domain of the CMS – and the two may or may not co-exist. Thus, you can get FDA approval and a negative coverage decision by Medicare. The real-world part of the equation also to consider is that the CMS is under a legislative mandate to be budget neutral, meaning that every dollar added means that one has to be subtracted elsewhere.

> Example: The Charite disc replacement is an example where the company (J&J) received FDA approval, but did not get the CMS ruling that it wanted. CMS DID in fact agree to cover the Charite disc (and disc replacement in general), but it ruled that it is 'equivalent' to existing treatments. Thus, they reimbursed at a rate equivalent to that of existing treatments, while the Charite disc was a premium product both in terms of price and in terms of surgeon OR time and training requirements. Thus, even though the product was intended primarily for a younger patient, the CMS ruling has had a dramatic impact on the commercial/ private insurers since they use CMS as a benchmark for relative valuation. Therefore, getting reimbursement and getting the right reimbursement can be two different things.

MEDICAL DEVICE MARKETING

After putting together a solid case for efficacy and reasonable for CMS, comes the hard part – getting each and every private insurer to make a positive coverage decision. Each one has either a Medical Director or Tech Review committee to review new technology/procedures and to determine whether it is beneficial for the insurance company to cover it. Keep in mind that in addition to medical information, it is in fact a company that you are talking to – they also want to do the 'right thing', but aren't going to pay for a technology or procedure because it helps a patient in 10-20 years, long after they have left their patient rolls. Most insurance company 'customers' turn over within 3-5 years; thus, they are looking for solid medical information that makes sense given the fact that they have to live with rising costs of technology and ever-increasing bureaucracy. This is where long-term and real-life may collide.

Types of questions that medical coverage review boards will ask in assessing 'why should we pay?' include:

- Effectiveness
- Reasonable to pay
- Necessity to pay
- No harm to the patient
- Scientifically proven, clinically valid
- U.S. versus global clinical studies (prefer U.S. in the U.S., but will accept outside the U.S. as long as study controls and data are solid)
- Other products/ competing alternatives currently on the market

If coverage is granted, the carrier will issue guidelines that provide specific details on exactly when, where, how, and who coverage applies to. These are generally issued in the form of recommendations based on their medical review, as well as guidelines for coverage. Below are standard items often included in these coverage reviews:

- Patient population – who intervention (procedure/technology) should be given to
- Protocol of use – how to give the intervention
- Timing of use – when
- Provider characteristics – what are the qualifications necessary in the healthcare provider for them to use the intervention safely and effectively
- Setting characteristics – where/ place
- Trade-off – benefits and harms as compared to alternatives.

The letter of the law

Have you heard of Advamed? Stark laws? If you've heard of these topics, then you may not need the following section...but if you haven't or you're not really sure what it all means, then read on to get a basic breakdown of the facts.

First – definitions...

- Advamed – is short for Advanced Medical Technology Association, and is a nonprofit group of medical device manufacturers that offers many services to its members, including (and perhaps especially) lobbying efforts. Typically, the term "Advamed" in conversation is a reference to the Advamed code of ethics/guidelines that all members agreed to follow in their dealings with healthcare professionals. The guidelines were updated at the end of 2008 from the first version drafted in 2006 and can be accessed at http://www.advamed.org/MemberPortal/About/code/. The purpose of these guidelines is to standardize and self-police the device industry, similar to that of the pharma companies, so that government intervention (including the DOJ) is minimized. Note that not all device manufacturers and distributors belong to Advamed. A company that does not belong may choose to 1) still sign the guidelines, 2) not sign but still follow, or 3) develop and follow their own guidelines. NOTE: There is nothing magical about the Advamed guidelines; it is the interactions between the company, sales force, and healthcare professional that count.
- Stark laws – named after Congressman Pete Stark, these laws are all about physicians referring patients to themselves, or rather preventing that practice, specifically Medicare and Medicaid patients. The idea is that if the physician can refer the patient to a place where he/she could financially gain, then there is a real potential for over-use or over-referral – which leads to fraud in the Medicare/Medicaid system. Thus, if a physician has ANY financial interest in an entity, he or she cannot refer patients there. The Stark law was first passed in 1989 and only covered lab services, but has since been extended several times to cover additional areas and become more stringent, with the newest additions taking effect October, 2009. More information can be found at http://starklaw.org.
- Anti-kickback statutes – while the Stark laws are civil statutes and thus mean financial compensation if there are violations, the anti-kickback statues are criminal laws and can carry a much harsher penalty. Both are

often referred to together, even though they are quite different. The broad brushstroke is that ANY kind of transaction (real or virtual) that induces a healthcare provider to select a product is prohibited. Any inducement to a healthcare provider to select a specific service, procedure, device, location, etc. is interpreted by the government as a type of bribe that then causes the cost of the physician's decision to be passed on via Medicare/Medicaid. Note that the OIG (Office of Inspector General) has been very clear that business practices acceptable in other industries are NOT alright with medical devices. Taking a surgeon to a sports game, sending a birthday gift, or even holding a training event at a "lavish" site are all inappropriate transactions between company personnel and the healthcare provider. Hospitals are also included under this statute and must keep their relationships with vendors at arms-length. Note that BOTH the healthcare provider and the company person can be held liable. Two good articles are listed below:

» http://foley.com/files/tbl_s31Publications/FileUpload137/5430/ct1108_OppenheimRosenberg.pdf - An Introduction to Federal Anti-Kickback Statute and Stark Law (Nov, 2008), 3 page review written by 2 lawyers

» http://www.orthosupersite.com/view.asp?rID=26715 – Orthopedists liable under federal anti-kickback statute: Surgeons who have agreements with companies should review their arrangements for compliance (2008).

VERY IMPORTANT side note – In 1997, Congress passed an amendment that allows the OIG to prosecute for civil penalties under the anti-kickback statues. Why is that important? Because they can get treble (3x) financial damages + $50,000 per incident and only have to prove "preponderance of evidence." When it comes to allocating government resources, it now makes real financial sense to dig deep into anti-kickback investigations. Bottom line – expect more, not less going forward.

So, what does this mean to me?

The answer is quite a bit. As you plan to launch a product, you now have to think hard about any giveaways. Education must meet compliance guidelines. Agreements with surgeons require particular scrutiny to ensure both parties continue to live up to their end of the contract on an ongoing basis. As a rule of thumb, keep in mind "fair market value" for all transactions with surgeons and hospitals. Ask this question: can you easily demonstrate that the relative value you/your company is getting in return for what you're paying?

As a company leader in marketing, you are responsible for assessing the need and the risk, and then making a recommendation on how to best use company resources going forward. Understanding of the laws and the possible penalties for your company, your customers, your sales team, and even for you personally is integral to a solid assessment and ultimately, a good decision.

Ethics and responsibility — is there a higher standard in medical devices? Should there be?

In some ways, this is a personal decision and reflects your own internal compass. However, there is an argument that to fully succeed in medical device marketing, putting the patient's needs first is not just a nice thing to do, but rather, it is a necessity. It is ultimately the patient's well-being that determines whether the healthcare provider/physician feels positive about using your product. In a nutshell, if making a difference in people's lives and making sure that your products are "right" is not a critical aspect of who you are, then medical device marketing may be a difficult road to travel. Here are some reasons why it is important:

- If your device fails, or simply doesn't work well in patients, then success is a struggle on every front.
- The surgeon/physician is the one who has to see the patient face-to-face, or get the page or phone call if there is a problem. An unhappy patient = an unhappy surgeon/physician = an unhappy customer = a lost customer?
- Often a critical selling tool to surgeons and physicians is clinical trial results. It is quite difficult to develop solid studies, interest surgeons, and then generate results unless the patient is the legitimate focus.
- Creditability (personal and company) is a key asset. With a customer who is focused on the patient and still balances business, your ability to do so as well can help you connect.

The bottom line is that medical devices are implanted for a long period of time, sometimes permanently, into the patient's body and most perform some critical function. Unlike clothing or toys or other consumer goods, the weight of responsibility is much higher because of what these parts are intended for. Above and beyond any regulation or law, your commitment to the patient and to do what is right is a critical aspect of the medical device industry. While

◄ **MEDICAL DEVICE MARKETING**

not in any textbook or even discussed as part of marketing, great medical device marketers know that their integrity, their company's reputation, and the trust of healthcare providers are on the line every product launch and with every product used. One question that seems to keep many on the right track is, "Would I be comfortable if this device was going into my mother or grandmother?"

CHAPTER 2

Building a Business Plan (and Controlling Your Destiny)

Once the research has been done and the market assessment is complete, a top-notch product manager stops to consider the question of: "Is this project the best use of company resources, right now or in the future?" It is the product manager's role to make this assessment and present both the data and a recommendation to the company. Ultimately, building a business plan requires not only bringing together and analyzing data, but also providing counsel and guidance on what path brings the most success in the face of all the internal and external variables.

Putting together a credible business plan requires the elements discussed in this chapter. Neglecting one area will not only weaken the plan, but may lead to a conclusion that leads to a poor choice. While there is no guarantee that doing every element thoroughly will lead to the correct decision, it is the product manager's job to ensure that all information available has been gathered, analyzed, and processed in light of the opportunity, the competition, and the resources available.

Market research: What, when, and how?

As with any type of market research, you can gather information from primary sources, market data, and research reports. In medical devices, gathering market research is a critical component to making good decisions, and yet it can be extremely difficult to find good information or sometimes to find any information at all. So, what are some sources to use? When do you use them? And how do you make the most of what information you have, especially when you don't have very much?

Primary Sources

First, primary sources are useful for two reasons: a) gathering basic information about a new area or market that you or your company is not familiar with and/or b) confirming a market assessment, particularly if the information is controversial or conflicts with other data. The issue with primary sources is that it is difficult to get a representative sampling of potential customers, especially since it is typically much easier to gather information from existing customers than a full representation of the market.

Also, developing a survey instrument that asks questions in an unbiased manner can be quite challenging, plus asking those questions without inadvertently tilting the results can be tough. There are several companies who will develop and administer surveys, and even analyze results. Some are full-service, while others will take questions already developed from several companies and set up a booth at a convention. They ask qualified convention participants the questions and then sort the results back to each company. Both of these options work well, as long as you have time and money. Count yourself especially fortunate if you work at a company that has a market research analyst (*really* lucky if you have an entire department) that can help you in developing questions, selecting a company to work with, and analyzing results.

Another source of primary data can be the focus group, and though the quantity of data is narrow, the quality is richer. This approach is used less often. These can be done formally or informally. The informal version is typically done with a small invited group of customers; these can be current, past, or potential customers. The meeting content and methodology for gathering information can be developed along a number of lines, but often it is centered around assessing technology and/or understanding where the market is likely to head in the future. A more formal focus group generally requires professional facilitation and analysis and is most often handled by a firm specializing in recruiting qualified candidates, developing a focus group format, and then running an anonymous discussion, or series of discussions. The effort and cost of holding focus groups limits their usefulness and how often they are held.

There are two other sources of primary information that should be routinely tapped. The first is the sales force. Not only do they have regular contact with current and potential customers, but also they see a variety of competitor devices and literature. Gathering data via surveys, e-mails, phone calls, or even small groups can be very helpful as either a first step or to validate/substantiate other data. Additionally, as a product manager develops contacts and relationships with people who work at other companies, it may be possible to directly gather competitive information on what is going on or where the market is headed.

Secondary sources

Secondary sources are much more readily available without the time and preparation needed for primary sources. There are several possible sources of data, although it is rare to find exactly the data needed without combining information from several sources and then making a determination as to what is correct. If a market research report has been written, these are often good sources of data about several related markets, with future predictions and competitor information. (A list of reputable research companies and contact information is in Chapter 8.)

Information can be mined from several databases, some of which are free and some require a subscription fee. Databases can be rich sources of information especially when working with someone who can extract and combine data strands in order to reveal new ways to look at the market, trends, or a different customer profile. The trick is making sure that you plan well enough to gather not only all the data you need, but in the format needed to merge and analyze. Care also should be taken to really understand that data sources, both actual data and trending assumptions, especially when looking at procedures or surgeon data which can be tricky to accurately assess in both the public and private sectors.

Another solid source of information of information would be financial analyst reports for a specific industry. Several firms have analysts that follow specific industries and issue reports that are solid sources of third-party data. Some analysts even produce reports following major meetings. Once you have familiarity with an analyst and know that he understands the industry and technology, then having a track record of reports from the same source is desirable in order to establish confidence and trend lines. A strong supplement to the analyst reports can be major competitor financial reports and even information from analyst meetings. If you dig deeper into the financial reports or analyst information, they sometimes contain information about product launches, as well as sales channel strategy and expenditure, possibly even some direction about future goals.

On the global front, the best bet for a holistic view is working with market reports that assess Europe, Australasia, and the Americas. It may take more than one report and require some integration and assessment of data in order to come up with a realistic market model. If available, gathering data from in-market channels and subsidiaries in order to compare and contrast market reports and to refine the information is desirable. Additionally, a couple of countries have registries that can be accessed via internal country contacts. Australia and

Sweden both have implant registries that provide usage information, although it is a year or more old. Japan also has a type of registry that comes out every couple of years. These registries can sometimes be obtained by local company contacts, but may require a local surgeon friend in order to obtain. Other countries may have partial or implant-specific registries, such as Canada with orthopaedic hip and knee implants. It is worth talking to local sources and find out if something exists.

A COUPLE OF MARKET RESEARCH CAVEATS...

First, developing a global market view requires parsing together several reports and sources and is typically difficult to do. Focusing on specific high-value, high-profile markets may be easier than trying to capture 'the world.' Coalescing various regional preferences into a business plan and market profile may require breaking a project scope into two, or even three, parts. Thinking through the numbers and the way surgery is done and distribution is handled in each country is required to accurately assess and reflect the market.

Second, numbers are at least one year behind the actual market, as well as being estimates made roughly a year in advance, which makes them 18-24 months out of date. So, when looking at an emerging market trend that is shifting *fast*, it is probably not reflected correctly anywhere. Gathering information on something new may require putting together secondary sources that are incomplete or behind the curve and then updating them with an assessment based on primary source input. This is tricky: documenting your assumptions and methodology for analysis is critical in presenting information. That way, someone can disagree with assumptions or methodology, which may impact the conclusion, but you aren't arguing whether data exists or not, which is when a product manager is on shaky ground.

A summary point is a rule of thumb -- not always true, but something to gauge the market by. When the surgeon asks for a specific device or modification, you are likely 6-12 months behind the market leader. When the sales force asks for a specific device or modification, you are likely 12-24 months behind. This is simply because once someone is asking for it, the idea generally springs from something seen or heard somewhere else. Surgeons often see and hear ideas (even second-hand) that competitors are working on prior to them hitting the market, while the sales team's awareness typically awakens as clinical/limited release starts. This is true even if the person or people can not pinpoint where the idea springs from. For some reason, the adage 'great minds think alike' holds true in devices and similar concepts will start appearing in unrelated venues.

Assessing opportunity: adding in the personal touch

It is very easy to become enamored of a project during the research phase, to be swayed by the ideas and the prospect of making a mark and launching a project, but the right course is to put away emotion and coolly view the resource drain, the timeframe (best case/worst case), the sales and profit scenarios, share and positioning impact, and return on investment.

A product manager who can assess a project reasonably and fairly as a business proposition and participate in an open discussion about "your" project versus others demonstrates a greater level of ability and value. It also helps if you have a good understanding of your company's product portfolio strategy and ROI metrics.

Some things to consider in assessing the opportunity:

For sales growth, the sales team needs a stream of product launches that support existing product lines and introduce new platforms. However, there is typically an 'absorption rate' for the sales team that has to be assessed and accounted for in order to maximize the impact of new products and get the most out of the investment. If too many products are launched in a short period of time, information overload sets in and either the sales force cherry picks or all the products suffer to some degree.

Additionally, marketing looks at the lifecycle of existing products, and in some arenas those lifecycles can be extended by refreshing or updating the platform with line additions or upgrades. Often these upgrades and additions don't look as good in a financial analysis and can be difficult to assess because it prevents customer loss or extends product lifecycles. While gathering information and putting together analyses can be difficult, these types of projects are relatively easy for the sales team to absorb and can keep sales growing while new platforms are developed. This is particularly true if the line add/ upgrade can apply to longer-term results and scientific data, allowing the company and the sales team to leverage technical and clinical data.

One of the most difficult assessments to make is when there is a quick market shift or trend that opens up a window of opportunity. It amounts to the task of being able to launch xyz product line addition within a short timeframe. When this happens, it is generally as the result of 1-2 competitors coming out with a gee-whiz device or gadget. It appears from primary customer data and sales channel input that this new gadget is making a significant market impact and the opportunity exists to a) scoop sales and share and b) be on the leading curve of product development.

This is not a huge project, but something that does require resources and expertise either internally or to purchase, and does so at the expense of another project. The question is – is it worth doing or not? The marketing textbooks say that the correct answer is not to deviate from strategic portfolio development and to simply consider whether it should be added when resources become available. The problem is that it is a 'right-now' hot product that requires immediate resources to meet goals a) and b) above. In real life, there is no absolute hard-and-fast rule or 100% *right* answer in making this decision. It may be worthwhile to deviate a bit and take advantage of the opportunity, as long as a few things can be reasonably determined (in your assessment/opinion):

1) Do you have the capability (either internal or external) to actually pull off a short timeframe project and launch it?
2) Is this 'gadget' a "flash in the pan" or a true marketplace shift? (In other words, is this something you're going to have to do anyway, and doing it now and quickly means that you take advantage of the shift instead of following much later with little net effect?)
3) Is the ability to scoop sales and market share real? Is it worth postponing another project in order to do this one from a dollar-and-cent perspective?

Financial analysis: putting your house in order

The key elements of a financial analysis are the same for virtually every project and across most companies, although each situation and firm may have different metrics to measure by. The purpose of this section is not to explain how to do a financial analysis or put numbers together, rather to touch on various elements that are often either overlooked or not handled well.

SALES

In developing the sales profile, there are a couple of things to keep in mind. First, build the financials in units to start with and then apply the dollars based on average sales price (ASP). This allows for a couple of things: a) list and ASP may vary by region or country and you can layer worksheets or make price changes easily if needed, b) it is easy to switch between implant and procedure volume if needed, c) cannibalization can be evaluated both on a unit and dollar level, and d) links between instrument sets and implants can be viewed and changed easily.

Cost of Goods

It is common practice for the cost of tooling to be amortized into implants for the first six months or a year of production. Cost can also vary as production standardizes and kinks are worked out, often going down but sometimes increasing. If production moves to outside vendors at a certain volume level or after a certain timeframe post-launch, costs can increase simply because production goes outside. While sometimes these can't be predicted, it is up to the product manager to know the most up-to-date information from the manufacturing team as well as any predictions, expectations and concerns on what is likely to happen and load this information into the financials.

Inventory

Developing the inventory plan can be a complex equation or relatively simple, depending on the number and type of implants/instruments, sales channel(s), replenishment planning process, along with supply-chain specific issues (i.e. loaners versus consignments). There are a few sometimes overlooked items to make sure you consider while developing inventory:

- Don't forget what is needed to actually sell and demonstrate the system – samples and demo/ workshop sets. Many companies put these items at the end of the manufacturing priority list, but devices need to be seen and handled in order to effectively launch them. Ensuring they are considered in the initial forecast gives manufacturing time to plan and you the leverage to push for completion/availability.
- Setting guidelines for how sets will be used – is it the same for implants and instruments? Not only should turn requirements be considered, but also implant usage and set allocations for high volume centers have to be taken into account. What about outliers? Are you using national loaners, regional loaners, or seed outlier sets throughout the sales channel? Will channel representatives return sets as required? In some companies, the penalties for NOT returning loaner sets is not very high, and thus sets run late or aren't returned at all. Could this be an issue? All these are items to assess and address *beforehand*.
- Replenishment during launch and pipeline fill are closely related, and tied tightly to the number of instrument sets as well. Predicting turns per set or usage per month is the product manager's job – yet the only fact that is 100% predictable is that the numbers will be wrong. The real question… and a test of the product manager's skill… is 'how wrong?' Knowing

how long the manufacturing cycle is and whether the suppliers hold any on-hand inventory can shorten the time-to-shelf cycle. Other critical factors are looking at existing and planned future usage and estimating the demand curve of sizes used. Information from prior launches, existing product sales, and input from sales channels all help, but ultimately, the initial stock quantity and replenishment manufacturing resources require a product manager's decision.

Assumptions		Year 1	Year 2	Year 3	Year 4	Year 5	Year 6	Year 7	Year 8	Year 9	Year 10
ASP per procedure		$4,200	$4,116	$3,993	$3,793	$3,755	$3,717	$3,680	$3,570	$3,463	$3,567
	Δ in ASP		-2%	-3%	-5%	-1%	-1%	-1%	-3%	-3%	3%
Average Procedures / Month / Set			2.2	2.3	2.3	2.2	2.1	2.0	1.9	1.7	1.5
	Quarter 1	0.5									
	Quarter 2	1.0									
	Quarter 3	1.5									
	Quarter 4	2.0									
# of Instruments in Field			200	260	300	335	365	400	420	400	370
	Quarter 1	10									
	Quarter 2	25									
	Quarter 3	50									
	Quarter 4	100									
Instrument Sets Costs		$10,283	$9,955	$9,920	$9,920	$9,920	$9,920	$9,920	$9,920	$9,920	$9,920
COGS per procedure		$840	$800	$770	$770	$770	$770	$770	$770	$770	$770
Commission		20%	20%	20%	20%	20%	20%	20%	20%	20%	20%
# of Implants in fielded sets		20									
Implant Set cost		$16,800									

	Year 1	Year 2	Year 3	Year 4	Year 5	Year 6	Year 7	Year 8	Year 9	Year 10
# of Procedures (based on turns/ instr)	915	5280	7176	8280	8844	9198	9600	9576	8160	6660
Sales (Procedures x ASP)	$3,843	$21,732	$28,650	$31,405	$33,209	$34,193	$35,330	$34,185	$28,256	$23,754
COGS (Procedure Cost)	$769	$4,224	$5,526	$6,376	$6,810	$7,082	$7,392	$7,374	$6,283	$5,128
Gross Margin	$3,074	$17,508	$23,125	$25,030	$26,399	$27,110	$27,938	$26,811	$21,973	$18,625
Gross Margin %	80.0%	80.6%	80.7%	79.7%	79.5%	79.3%	79.1%	78.4%	77.8%	78.4%
Cost of sales (commissions)	$769	$4,346	$5,730	$6,281	$6,642	$6,839	$7,066	$6,837	$5,651	$4,751
Launch costs	$1,000	$500	$250							
Incremental sets per year	100	100	60	40	35	30	35	20	0	0
Instrument set inventory - incremental	$1,028	$996	$595	$397	$347	$298	$347	$198	$0	$0
Implant set inventory - incremental	$1,680	$1,680	$1,008	$672	$588	$504	$588	$336	$0	$0
Net Margin	($1,403)	$9,986	$15,542	$17,680	$18,822	$19,470	$19,937	$19,440	$16,322	$13,875
Net Margin %	-36%	46%	54%	56%	57%	57%	56%	57%	58%	58%

Project scope: figuring out what is in and what is out

Determining the size and direction of the project is like putting pieces of a puzzle together - some parts come from customer input; some from assessing future market trends; some from planning differentiation strategy, and some from integrating it with the company's competencies and resources. The farther into the project you go, the easier it is to clearly see the final picture of what the product will be, and what it won't be as well. However, to truly be a leader within the product manager role and to stay on time and within budget for a project, the project scope must be clearly articulated and committed to early in the business planning process. Even though the 'picture' may not be complete, the outline for what is 'in scope' and what is 'out of scope' has to be clean, well defined, and stable.

The idea of defining the scope of a project sounds relatively simple, assuming you've done your market research and can define the state of the market and the particular segment and customers targeted. Then the project scope should start out as a fairly straightforward statement of what the product needs to accomplish and why. As the business plan progresses and customer input is better defined (often called the 'user needs' phase) and engineering terminology more cleanly states must-have, nice-to-have, don't-need aspects, then the scope becomes even more solid. In addition, the marketing message/differentiation strategy should also be clear.

At this point, the idea is to STOP – the market is defined, the customer target is defined and needs and desires have been elucidated. Also, an outline of a value proposition with positioning statment and a differentiation message should exist. The project scope is *done* and the development team is entirely focused on execution with a clear view of the entire team toward time and dollar metrics.

The stage gate process: step-by-step from concept to launch

Hopefully, your company already has a stage-gate process, otherwise known as a project planning/ development process or business-project reviews. However, there are companies that don't – and there are also companies that have the process but don't use it well. This section breaks down a concept-to-launch stage gate review into a generic version and touches on key issues from a business marketing perspective.

It is the product manager's job to ensure that complete information is put together and to drive the project proposal through the steps from a business perspective. Whether the business plans are reviewed by an executive team or by some other committee, having accurate data for decision making and planning is critical to both the company's finances and to developing your reputation.

Step One: Product Concept and Business Overview

This is sometimes a pre-gate stage review and is done to determine whether the project/product idea should have company resources devoted to it. In order to make this decision, there are two key parts that should be examined.

- The first is on the technical side: is the idea something that the company is willing and/or able to do? This doesn't mean it is easily doable, although far less resources and fewer capabilities are required if it is relatively straightforward technically from a development and manufacturing perspective. If it is technically challenging, then the company has to commit far greater resources and generally a much

longer timeline to the project to bring it to fruition. The assessment, however, needs to outline company competency as well as resources and needs from a technical perspective in order to complete the project successfully.
- The second aspect is determining if the opportunity is rich enough, especially in consideration of the resources required. An overview of the market from a macro perspective, both of size and growth, is needed. Then break that out into the relevant segment(s) under consideration. Both industry market dynamics (competitors, market shifts, etc.) and external dynamics (reimbursement, regulatory, etc.) should be given some consideration, enough to be able to pinpoint where likely risks/minefields may lie and determine if there's a market position available for exploitation. A four-square diagram that gives 2-axis critical to the market and plots competition versus the market position under consideration is an ideal way to highlight the opportunity from a marketing perspective. The business case at this stage should be at roughly a 50% confidence interval – information in some areas may be sparse or missing and sales profit projections may be 'guess-timates'. However, enough data should be available with critical informational analysis highlighted to allow a solid review of the opportunity at hand.

Goal: To allow marketing, development, and other indirect resources to be allocated to the project in order to build a project team, develop-user needs profiles, validate market positioning, and to confirm and further build a business case to a 65-75% confidence level.

Step Two: Develop Team and User Needs

During the second phase of the process, the plan as outlined in step one is taken apart and re-processed to a) add information to incomplete sections and b) validate that the data is correct. Step One is a preliminary review in many ways and shouldn't be unduly burdened – completing the information in a relatively quick timeframe and making reasonable assessments are important so the best business propositions rise to the surface and are resourced. However, it is during the second phase that the real work on the project begins and at the end of Step Two, confidence must be fairly high that the information is complete and the go-forward plan is well laid out.

- Build project team – the internal team and external team members need to be identified. For the internal team, determining who is on the team and holding the first meeting to outline the project and the expected need for resources is an important part of getting full company participation in

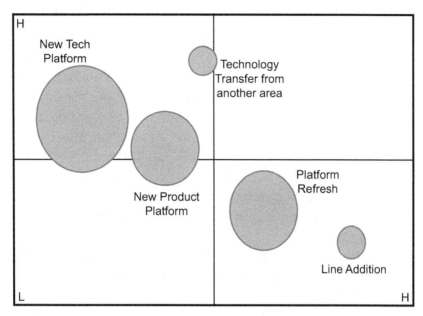

Bubble Size – Represents Market Size

the project. Additionally, every department has to be aware and involved during early timeline discussions; otherwise, critical tasks and dates will be missed. If used, the external team of consultants also has to be put together during this timeframe. Developing a team dynamic that balances the consultants' expertise with the company's engineering and business expertise can make or break a project – it takes collaboration between the product manager and lead engineer to run design team meetings that are effective with a healthy exchange of ideas across the clinical and business management spectrum.

- Develop user needs – while the phase one business plan outlines the market and the opportunity, it is during phase two that a detailed picture of exactly *what* the project will be and won't be is developed. This information has to be gathered in two forms in order for it to be fully usable – and unfortunately, it is typically only gathered in one format, often leading to project scope issues later on. Both pieces of information go hand-in-hand to gain a full scope, but it is not always intuitively obvious what is needed. It is then up to the product manager to really analyze, dig, and bring the experience of others in to crystallize the data. The first form of user needs is the engineering design input that often comes out in the form of lists of need-to-have, nice-to-have, and don't need categories.

These design parameters translate into where the project is heading from an actual nuts-and-bolts perspective – and gets translated into the inputs-outputs page of the design file notebook. It is often where the user needs phase ends. However, it leaves out the important understanding of how this information fits into the market positioning – the who, when, why and where that goes along with the 'what' part of user needs. Once the user needs data has been gathered, the information also needs to shape the market positioning into the 2-3 key benefits and specific message. While this may not be the final version, a preliminary version at this stage gives you and the team a clear picture of the market opportunity as well as the chance to test conversion concepts and real-life scenarios as the project moves forward.

- Validate market positioning – while building the external development team (if needed) and/or talking with current or potential customers in creating the user needs matrix, provides the chance to fully populate and check the market dynamics and the game plan to capture share. While primary and secondary source data remains the core elements of market research, the medical device arena often has underlying market dynamics based on technology and innovation, or even reimbursement. This may not be fully captured in older data. Thus, getting a first-hand sense of the market stability, trends, and emerging segments can be invaluable in developing sales and forecast projections.

Goal: Present a solid design review and business plan based on user needs and market positioning. Confirm/revise sales and profit within agreed upon timelines and request specific resources needed for entering clinical trials. Confidence interval at the end of Step Two should be 75-85%.

Step Three: Clinical Trials

The product manager role during this phase is two-fold...first, to validate that the product developed will meet the sales and profit target, and second, to test the market launch message and plan. There is also an ancillary role of communicating with the sales force on what is going on – who will get sets, when, for how long, how training will be conducted, problem-solving, etc. That, in itself, can easily subsume the product manager's time. Be careful – this is NOT the product manager's key task during this time, although communication within the development team and the sales force to ensure the project is on track and everyone is on the same page IS important. Just be careful that you prioritize the less urgent, but ultimately more important functions of validating financials and messaging so that they get done.

- Validate that the product will meet sales and profit targets. To meet this goal, the product manager has to know ahead of time who the conversion targets are, based on the market opportunity/positioning plan. Then, the clinician panel/trial typically needs to be broken into at least 2 parts:
  » The first is for the design team surgeons to make adjustments to the instruments or implants based on user need criteria. This is a fundamental check of product performance and to ensure that all parts work correctly as they were designed, plus make any tweaks needed to maximize effectiveness. This may be a limited release launch into surgery or can take place at a few cadaver labs where surgery is simulated.
  » While this second, larger-scale clinical trial is sometimes overlooked or ignored, either to speed the product to market or because it is not seen as necessary, it is absolutely critical to confirming non-developer surgeon input and putting together accurate forecasts. The second stage involves targeting non-customers that meet a pre-specified conversion profile. While it is ideal if these non-customers do have some relationship with the company beforehand so that information flows easily, it is this part of the clinical trials that gives real confidence in predicting sales and profit – both from a tangible perspective of seeing conversions happen and understanding the how's and whys (plus any issues) in the conversion process. Additionally, the 'stories' of sales successes provide psychological boosts that fuel the sales team during the launch.
- Test market/ launch message and plan – having not only a draft surgical technique, but also draft sales sheets, ad campaign outline, and perhaps even a rough design rationale provides an opportunity to validate that the benefits outlined in the planning phase truly appeal to the market. The *market* includes the surgeons, OR staff, and potentially even hospital buyers and purchasing committees. Before finalizing the conversion process – both the key messages and the steps in the process – use the clinical trials to determine whether the material you put together is relevant and useful. Actual participation in sales calls (if possible) in addition to soliciting representative feedback not only increases your personal creditability, but also truly helps to construct a well thought-out and sturdy sales funnel plan for marketing support material.
- Sales team communication – while being the liaison between the sales team and manufacturing/ development is a critical function during this

phase, there is a balance that must be achieved in spending time on this function versus the previous two. Part of the product manager's role is to ensure that the sales team knows in advance that a surgeon in their territory is part of the clinical trial, when he/she will receive an instrument/ implant set, and the expectations of the representative and the surgeon in terms of communicating input. Surgeon and sales representative training is also sometimes needed prior to product use; this is something with which the product manager is also involved , although it is absolutely critical to pull in resources from the education/ meeting planning team, in addition to working with the development engineers and design surgeons to pull these sessions together. Regardless of the number of tasks, amount of communication, or complexity of involvement, the product manager has to be constantly aware of the percentage of time dedicated to the sales team and ensure the first two tasks are taking precedence. If needed, pull in other corporate resources in planning and executing the sales team's communication and training.

Goal: Determine that the product developed is both safe and effective in patient treatment and meets goals set out in project plan, specifically user needs, cost targets, and customer conversion targets. Business plan should confirm sales/ profit projections at an 85 - 95% confidence interval and focus should primarily be on launch plan and timeline, including clear discussion of any risks and resource issues that need executive intervention. Gain approval for launch execution, including building inventory and budget for launch sales package. (NOTE: This is usually a large $$ approval gate and may receive increased scrutiny – be prepared to answer questions and defend numbers, even if plans slid through before.)

Step Four – Product Launch

What is product launch? The exact definition is a hotly debated topic in many companies – even though it is the end goal of most projects and generally comprises metrics in bonus calculations. While there can be as many legitimate definitions as there are companies, the following is proposed as a working classification, both for the purposes of this book and in case you want to propose it to start conversation at your company:

> *Product launch: At the end of Stage 2 (75-85% confidence level), the number of sets forecasted for launch are locked in as the official <u>launch quantity</u>. The marketing plan is also outlined in terms of education, sales support material, clinical studies, etc. at the same time. Launch occurs when all of the forecast sets and*

BUILDING A BUSINESS PLAN (AND CONTROLLING YOUR DESTINY)

the elements of the marketing plan have been delivered. Until this point, launch has <u>not</u> occurred, even if ninety percent or more of the sets are operational; this is because financial metrics are built on a start date of <u>all</u> sets and lost sales cannot be made up.

Missing sets/ slow roll out at the beginning of a launch causes a loss of the <u>last</u> month's sales, not the <u>first</u> month's sales. See graphs below for a visual explanation for clarification. However, this is a very important point, because you are not just pushing the first months' sales out for one to two months, you are actually losing the last one to two months' sales when you miss the launch. The lost sales amount is MUCH greater when looked at this way- the correct way.

	Launch Plan - # of sets	Actual Launch - # of sets	Sales per set - Plan ($000's)	Cumulative Sales - Plan	Actual ($000's)	Cumulative Sales - Actual
March	20	0	100	100	0	0
April	20	20	200	300	100	100
May	20	20	300	600	200	300
June	20	20	400	1000	300	600
July	10	20	450	1450	400	1000
August	10	10	500	1950	450	1450
September	10	10	550	2500	500	1950
October	10	10	600	3100	550	2500
November	10	10	650	3750	600	3100
December	0	10	650	4400	650	3750

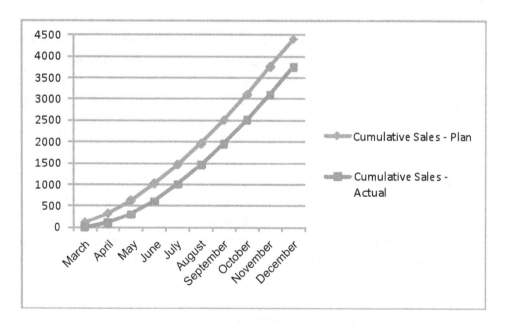

◄ MEDICAL DEVICE MARKETING

The significance of this definition is its requirement of every part of the company to work together and to be accountable for their respective areas in order for launch to be achieved. Not only must the required number of sets be delivered, but marketing also has to produce the launch material, development must assist both manufacturing and marketing in ensuring the launch occurs, and the other departments must fulfill their obligations as well.

There are three critical aspects of launch that the product manager should carefully orchestrate well ahead of the actual launch in order for it to run smoothly. Additionally, staying on top of these details during the launch (for between 4 and 12 months) is also important to meeting project goals. (Note that this is NOT a complete list of everything that needs to be done, but the highlights.)

- Sales funnel and set distribution plan – in some larger organizations, the product manager is not as hands-on and does not handle this function; however, in many companies, it is the product manager that prioritizes where sets are placed and thus is responsible for ensuring that set usage meets forecast. To effectively perform this function, the product manager must know where sets are going and what is in the sales funnel from the perspective of what is going on the prospect/ target/ conversion/ percentage close sales cycle . It also means establishing rules for how many turns/ sets are required for consignment versus loaners to maximize utilization.
- Data supporting product use – while the right message targeted to the right customer segment is the best way to drive clarity and consistency in positioning the product and capturing market attention, the medical device audience will require data in order to fully capitalize on sales potential. Data can be of three main types: bench testing/ lab support, clinical data from patients, and cost effectiveness/ efficiency studies to demonstrate benefit to the healthcare system. While development and testing engineers are invaluable in data development, it is the product manager who must survey the product benefits and the likely obstacles to sales and then sit with the engineering, testing, and clinical affairs teams to mine for potential data. Note that this function is an ongoing aspect of product management and does not end once the launch phase has finished; publication/ presentation planning should be an annual, semi-annual, or even quarterly part of the product manager's role for every major product line.
- Sales support material – there are some core pieces that are part of the OR training information package and standard for every launch (i.e.

surgical technique); however, each additional piece of the sales support package should serve a specific and targeted function in the sales cycle. In order to plan and deliver an effective sales support package, the product manager has to map-out a sales funnel based on the product benefits, market opportunity, and targeted customers, and then test the funnel steps in the real-world via consultation with members of the sales team and/or during the clinical trial. Mapping a sales cycle, or even multiple sales chains, and then building the sales package to match will minimize unused pieces and leave budget dollars available for other items.

- Other – there can be significant work required for an education plan for surgeons and/or sales representatives; sometimes this can even be a certification program needed prior to product use. Also, if the product launch is a major one, an advertising campaign that may involve interactive media, large conference attendance, or even direct-to-consumer interaction can be implemented. Any of these activities require a significant amount of planning and budget to effectively pull off and must be considered well in advance.

Goal: Implement launch as outlined in business plan, including set rollout and all marketing/ sales campaign backed up by data series and publication/ presentations as outlined. Measure number of customers (cannibalized, new, lost) and number of sets, turns per set per month, and complaints each month and compare against plan.

Step Five – Post Mortem Review

At approximately six months post-launch, it is a good idea to conduct a post-mortem review of the entire project from start up through current date. The purpose of this review is two-fold:

- First and most importantly, to assess whether the project is meeting the sales, inventory, customer, and profit goals as outlined in the business plan. While it is early in the product lifecycle, any issues can be identified and steps taken to address/ adjust based on either improving sales or reducing inventory.
- Second, a full-scale project review from the beginning allows identification of both things that could be improved and best-in-class actions/ ideas that can be incorporated into other projects or teams.

Goal: Assess whether the plan was executed as anticipated and whether the results are occurring as expected. Make decisions on any plan alterations going forward that are needed to better achieve goals.

CHAPTER 3

Product Development: Managing Issues and Meeting Deadlines

While the business plan captures the "what," "when," and "how" blueprint, it is the project development process in which the real heart and soul of product is shaped. For an effective product manager to be at the center of the project and really grasp the key technical aspects, involvement in the development process is required.

However, the product manager's role in development has to remain focused on the market, including the entire continuum of surgeons and not just those represented in the design team. It can be difficult to be involved in the development meetings, planning sessions, and discussions, and to balance input on technical aspects of the product design with an overall perspective of what is going to generate sales and profit for the company. This may mean intervening in a technical discussion on the "perfect" design that increases inventory by 300 percent to raise concerns over how the additional parts can confuse OR staff, cause issues within hospital storage, and limit the number of sets the company can produce due to increased cost. Your role at times is to be the mediator to expand perspective and bring in other points of view so that good decisions are made during development and the end product is one that has broad-based market appeal.

Project definition…and the creep to watch out for…

As part of the business plan, the project scope is defined. However, as the project progresses, a dilemma arises in virtually every large-scale project. As the development team's creativity and inspiration is sparking and information about the customer/market continues to pour in, perhaps even more freely than while doing research, the temptation to allow scope creep starts.

First, in small steps, just an additional instrument or a couple more sizes of implants, and then suddenly the underlying project dynamics have shifted. Perhaps it is the realization that with only a few tweaks, a whole new customer segment could be reached. Perhaps it is an understanding that there is another layer of customer needs that was not fully recognized and could be included without radical change. Perhaps it is simply the finding that the requests/ needs from customers are resulting in a much higher cost in instruments/ inventory than planned. Whatever it is, the temptation is to allow for just a *little bit more*- modify this project and still meet deadlines and cost targets.

Here's the truth: 90 percent of the time, you *can't*. No matter how *easy* it looks, scope creep costs time and money. Trying to cram more into the time, space, resources allotted will end up with something falling through the cracks or simply missing dates. So, does this mean that scope creep is always bad?

Generally, yes, scope creep is bad. If, during a project, additional information is discovered that could be used to develop a better version, expand customer appeal, or even reposition the device in the market place, then look carefully to determine whether a Part B should be added with its own business plan, resources, and financial justification. Occasionally, the new information discovered may mean that the project should be re-evaluated and a new project initiated with its own resources and a more complete project scope incorporating the new info.

It does not reflect poorly on the product manager/ project leader when new information and ideas surface during the course of the project because the company has entered a new arena and/or forged new relationships, and thus is simply learning and being exposed to more things. However, if surprise information and market needs are the norm, then there is a question of whether the market research has been done thoroughly enough or whether the person doing the analysis truly understands the market. The take-away is: good research and planning on the front-end minimize scope issues; but be aware of the danger of scope creep and recognize that sometimes it is inevitable. When the inevitable happens, look at the information objectively and decide whether it is really worth the risk to allow project creep or whether it is better to add a second tier or even initiate another project.

Financial targets or dart throwing with expertise...

An important part of meeting profit projections and maximizing the number of instrument/ implant sets the company produces is setting cost targets for instruments and implants. However, it is not uncommon for product managers to rely on the development and manufacturing teams to simply estimate probable costs and then use those estimates as the baseline. While this may be an acceptable method, particularly if the project is similar to another product, there are some inherent risks and alternative methods to consider.

First, while pricing should be determined by the market, cost is determined by a combination of practical considerations (material used, manufacturing overhead) and decisions made during the design process (number of items, complexity/ moving parts). Thus, getting information from the development and manufacturing team is important, but is not necessarily the final word. Rather, setting targets based on input from the team and with profit needs in mind can help shape decisions during the development process. For instance, instrument complexity may be pared down or the number of implants may be affected in order to meet cost targets. Alternatively, location of manufacturing and manufacturing techniques can impact cost. Either way, without cost targets, profit can quickly be eaten away. The necessary decisions to reduce cost will not be made when the possibility to make profits exists.

Physician input – when it is good and when it is not so hot

Getting physician input during a project is often seen as the Holy Grail; what a customer says, what a customer wants, what a customer needs is the end-all and be-all for the development team. However, the product manager should take a step back from customer input and seriously consider input from observation as well as from more than simply one physician or even one group/ segment of physicians. One rule of thumb when gathering input from the field is:

> Once you receive a specific request from a physician/ customer, you are about one year behind the competition, and a request from a sales representative indicates you are about two years behind the competition.

Note that for product line extensions or product updates/ refresh projects, this may not be an issue since the goal is essentially 'keeping up with the Joneses' and possibly adding an innovative twist. However, for a true platform project, the goal is typically to have some significant advancement above current technology, if not completely leapfrog the market. This requires advanced voice-of-customer listening and observation skills, which includes significant analysis and critical judgment.

Getting input and staying ahead

So, how can you get customer input (or sales input for that matter) and be ahead of the competition? First, there are physicians and customers out there who really lead in seeing future possibility. Identifying who they are and aligning with them not only provides insight and enables you to ask questions and consider possibility, but also it may give you a designer/ developer who brings a different, valuable perspective. There are also industry personnel who have been involved in a specific market for a long time and have developed instincts for the market. These people also bring ideas forward for consideration and can thoroughly assist in developing format and content for brainstorming sessions, product pipeline meetings, or even market research plans.

The trick in working with forward-thinking customers and internal personnel is cultivating honest conversation that still allows for critical analysis. There also has to be a willingness to listen and think about 'out-there' ideas that may seem too far in the future or simply too weird to consider. Sometimes these ideas can be refined or paired with another concept to bring something innovative to life. Another way to wade through 'out there' product concepts- especially if several of them address similar indications- is to allow some limited product development and see if one emerges as a viable contender. While not common, it has happened that competing projects have been taken all the way into clinical trials before determining where to go forward. Of course, the market opportunity has to justify the resource expenditure for this type of situation.

What if you do not have a forward-thinking customer/ physician or an industry expert in your arsenal to brainstorm with? How do you 'think forward' or leapfrog then? One of the most tried-and-true methods to stimulate innovation is to gain customer input via careful and controlled observation; to parse into the frustrations, time and resource- wasters; and even to look at behind-the-scene interactions to find fertile ground for product ideas that other companies do not see.

Note that observation includes not just the OR but also the clinical setting, and that sometimes talking to those around the customer/ user may uncover key opportunities as well. Why don't other companies see these same opportunities? The answer is: because they are most often engaged only in talking with the customer to get his/her input. However, true customer observation would yield a much more rich and dynamic experience in which you can glean information and then use it to initiate new conversations.

Getting customer input is a great way to defend decisions and determine the course of action going forward. However, it also can be an excuse for simply playing it safe and not really taking chances. The product manager has to determine *how* to get real input – whether from market research, conversations, observation, etc. – and *when* to apply that input – should you take every piece of information equally or prioritize? – in order to bring real value to the company.

FDA approval and reimbursement...behind the scenes

How does the product manager intersect with these two functions? How much expertise do you need, and what responsibility do you have for ensuring success? These questions can solicit a variety of answers, depending on the size of the company, internal departments already in place, and the historical role of the product management team in your firm. However, regardless of the answers, some level of awareness and enough expertise to reasonably interact with regulatory and reimbursement professionals is a good idea to be able to lead the business.

REGULATORY

Getting regulatory approval can be a long and arduous process, or it can be relatively simple, depending on the type of device and the specific country regulations. Many products are developed primarily for one country or region and then launched in secondary countries/ regions in order to maximize sales and profit. Building the development file along with scientific, and sometimes clinical, evidence is important for gaining regulatory approval under multiple rules.

In addition to gaining initial approval, there can be a follow-up requirement for ongoing clinical surveillance in order to confirm safety and efficacy of the device. This is a requirement in an increasing number of cases in Europe particularly, and is anticipated to grow even further. The incremental cost of the post-market surveillance is quite high, and the goal is generally to avoid it if at all possible, although voluntary post-market surveillance in the form of studies may take place anyway.

One positive in the regulatory world is that under the U.S.-Australia Free Trade Agreement and in collaboration with the EMEA (the E.U. equivalent of the FDA), a pilot project to more freely release information on medical device approval began in 2009. The purpose of this collaboration is to allow manufacturing certification in one country/ region to suffice across others and potentially to significantly reduce the documentation needed to clear a device approved in one country/ region for marketing in the others.

First, getting a product on the market requires clearing regulatory hurdles of safety and efficacy. While every country has its own guidelines, the two most commonly referenced regulatory agencies are the FDA and the EMEA. Both groups classify devices into Class I, Class II, and Class III. Though they each have a bit different criteria for how the classification breaks down, it basically falls into higher risk devices in higher categories, thus subject to stricter scrutiny. For instance, instruments used in surgery are typically Class I while implants will fall into Class II or Class III.

In order to put a device on the market in Europe, the manufacturer must first self-certify that they are in compliance with ISO standards related to manufacturing and device testing. Also, most devices must obtain a Declaration of Conformity by a European Notified Body. Once these requirements are met, the device must be labeled with the CE mark and can be marketed in all European countries.

In the U.S., devices that are Class I can be marketed as long as the manufacturer has notified the FDA and meets GMP (Good Manufacturing Practices) standards related to manufacturing, branding, labeling, etc. However, Class II and Class III devices require additional FDA interaction. The FDA requires 510k documentation for Class II devices on product development, all testing data, and any relevant information known about related or similar devices showing safety and efficacy. Class III devices require a PMA (Pre-Market Approval) that includes all the previous data plus a human clinical trial. (Note: Regulatory agencies are requiring clinical data more and more often and a Class II device may have an easier or faster path to market if supported by data. This is not always an option, but may be worth considering if possible.)

Time-to-market and costs increase exponentially as a device goes up the Class curve. A Class I device can be released virtually immediately, while a Class II device averages 60 to 120 days to go through the regulatory process. In contrast, a Class III device takes from two to five years on average to complete the human clinical trial and requires millions to cover the cost of data collection and analysis. In the market analysis and project scope phase of business planning, great care must be taken to understand where the device is likely to fall on the regulatory continuum in order to predict resource consumption and time-to-market.

NOTE: If a device that is already on the market has a change or addition that impacts/ affects the parameters of the initial regulatory testing, documentation, and paperwork, this usually requires a new 510k or some more extensive documentation/ justification which must be filed and reviewed. However, if the change/ addition is minor and stays within the previous testing/ information already reviewed by the FDA, then a notification only, called a 'letter to file,' may be all that is required.

> Update on the TGA - EMEA - FDA pilot project to rationalize international GMP inspection activities. (2009). Retrieved from www.tga.gov.au/international/ecmra0901.htm on Jan 15, 2009.
>
> U.S.-Australia free trade agreement: How U.S. companies can benefit. (n.d.). Export.gov. Retrieved February 1, 2009 from

PRODUCT DEVELOPMENT: MANAGING ISSUES AND MEETING DEADLINES

http://www.export.gov/fta/australia/index.asp.

Reimbursement

This section primarily applies to the U.S., although gaining or improving reimbursement outside the U.S. is possible as well. However, the mechanics for doing so outside the U.S. also requires gathering of information regarding cost and efficacy of the device, and then applying to the appropriate government agency. In some cases, a private insurance system must be addressed as well. Since similar mechanics are parts of the U.S. system, understanding the complexities of U.S. reimbursement is a solid basis for grasping international reimbursement issues as well.

Assessing a device's reimbursement potential and then planning for future needs has to take place early enough in the process that information can be gathered if needed to support a bid to change reimbursement. The time to assess whether or not current reimbursement is sufficient is during Phase 1 of the development process and during the planning stage in Phase 2. Information is then gathered to support reimbursement during Phase 3, when clinical trials are taking place. If planning hasn't taken place to correctly identify what type of data is needed during the clinical

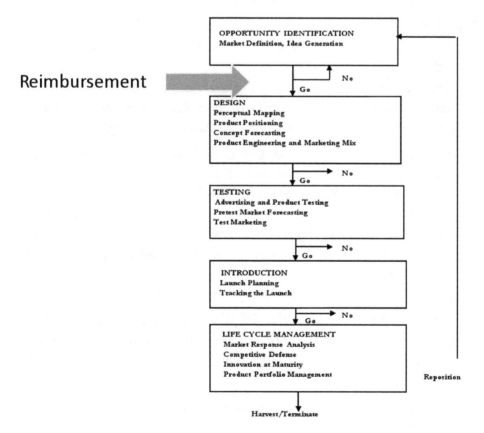

45

MEDICAL DEVICE MARKETING

trial, then your reimbursement argument will be weak and likely will not qualify.

Do I need a new code?

Below is a quick guide/ checklist to help in thinking through the issue of whether the technology/ procedure/ treatment is going to require a new code:

Step 1: What is the regulatory path?

A 510k usually uses existing codes and thus falls into established reimbursement amounts as well. However, a PMA may need a new code, and reimbursement information must be gathered during a PMA study in order to make the economic justification case.

Step 2: From where is reimbursement going to come?

Is this primarily a CMS (Medicare/ Medicaid) or private insurance patient? What studies are being done (or are planned), and what do they prove in terms of *effectiveness*? Who benefits, and against what comparison/ control? In what setting is this treatment/ procedure/ technology delivered (office, hospital, ASC, etc.)? Do existing codes describe the procedure? Is the $$ coverage adequate now?

Step 3: A new code is needed. What next?

If a new ICD-9 (diagnosis or procedure) code is required, then it might still fit into an existing DRG and thus ease the process through CMS. However, you will still have to go to every private carrier for their coverage decision. Be aware that there is great difficulty in gaining an *increase* in reimbursement if the code already fits within a DRG grouping.

If a new CPT (surgeon payment) code is required, this is controlled by the medical specialty societies and the AMA-CPT committee. While it does help in gaining coverage to get these codes, it is more difficult to get a higher RVU valuation because to do so will take money away from an existing procedure/ service. This means that these committees are essentially voting to take money out of the budget of a procedure/ service they are currently performing to put it into a new procedure/ service – not an easy sell. This is a zero-sum game – and thus, politics are a reality.

A new DRG code is a BIG DEAL. This requires time, studies, and economics justification – and do not forget the politics. There are no guarantees of success. It is not an impossible dream, but a difficult one.

Step 4: Moving forward

If you are going forward with a new code, there are a couple of rules to keep in mind.

First, get a new code for *procedure* or *treatment*, not for a product, particularly if you are looking to make a case for increased $$.

Second, get an expert to help you with the when, where, how strategy and the tactical execution of getting a code, setting up a study, etc. How things are set up in the beginning can make a huge difference in the end, and it is worth the investment.

MAKING THE BIGGEST IMPACT

Some hard-learned truths about reimbursement to keep in mind:

- Think short-term in planning studies. Long-term takes too long to prove, and the results may not be as relevant to commercial insurers. (Remember how quickly their customer population turns over…)
- There is no substitute for published evidence or for studies. A picture and data truly are worth a thousand words.
- Surgeon and hospital advocates, as well as government lobbying influence, make a difference. These types of people can talk to people and say things that you cannot.
- The heart of healthcare economics – can you come up with a way to capture and demonstrate cost savings as a result of the treatment/ technology/ service/ procedure?

REIMBURSEMENT AND THE MARKETING PLAN

In addition to outlining the fundamental reimbursement strategy based on all the analysis (from above), the marketing plan should also address the value proposition. This is key to the company's need to invest both the money and the additional time needed to deal with reimbursement issues.

The value proposition in reimbursement may be straightforward in the main part of the marketing plan and during presentations, but there should be thought and effort put into the value proposition for *every* stakeholder. This may be held in some appendix, but will likely be referenced and perhaps refined more than once as the project unfolds. The critical thought process – and potential stumbling block – is ascertaining what the value/ benefit will be for each stakeholder. Fundamentally, if there's no WIFM (i.e., they don't get paid or are paid less), then the market value will not be what it could/ should.

So, who are the stakeholders to consider?

- Surgeon/ physician
- O.R./ clinicians/ office (surgeon/ physician support staff)
- Hospital administration
- Patients
- Payers – public (CMS)/ private
- FDA
- Sales representatives

Other things to consider in putting together the marketing plan:

- Will speed to market be impacted by reimbursement? Does the organization have time/ patience? Is a slower speed justifiable?
- Conversely, will adoption rates/ barriers to entry be higher if reimbursement is not addressed?
- Could addressing reimbursement provide a competitive advantage/ barrier?
- Given current reimbursement, market pricing, and the cost to produce, can the treatment/ technology/ procedure make money if increased reimbursement does not happen? Is higher reimbursement an absolute requirement?
- What potential studies can be developed to address healthcare economics? What is the best control for comparison against in the study?

Managing issues/ meeting deadlines – or what to do when it all starts to fall apart

The perfect plan with complete dedication from the team sounds like a dream come true…and will still result in something at some point going wrong. Whether it is a design not testing out, a vendor not meeting deadline, FDA approval taking longer than planned, or even the clinical trials going more slowly than anticipated, there will be some kind of monkey wrench thrown into the works. The question really is: how do you handle it? Is it an excuse or a challenge? Or could it depend on what it is?

One of the first things to establish is that driving for results (i.e., delivering the product outlined in the business plan on time) is what a product manager is expected to do. If the product manager does not take on that responsibility as an owner of their business line, then there is a lack of leadership, particularly when things get off track. However, it should also be noted that the product manager also has an ethical responsibility regarding product safety that transcends all else.

During the project, various obstacles will arise. Some will be due to resource allocation (or the lack thereof), others due to prioritization or simply lack of focus, and still others because the sense of urgency or willingness to explore 'out-of-the-box' alternatives is not there. In dealing with these issues, both tactical and political questions come up – meaning who has the authority to decide? Should the question/ issue get executive attention/ review (even though or especially when someone might not "look good" during the review)? Can an exception be made to a policy/ procedure in order to meet a deadline? The organization as a whole can get tied into knots over these issues, with chain-of-command and concern over political fallout keeping issues from surfacing and problem-solving from taking place.

The product manager's role is to step in and intervene – to highlight the issue and mediate, bring it to an executive review, force a policy/ procedure exception decision, raise the questions of resources and prioritization so that clear decisions are made. While this may not make anyone happy – especially since no one will agree that you have the official authority to do so – it is generally accepted in most organizations that marketing's focus on meeting sales and profit goals means that taking direct aim at problems is in fact within the product manager's arena. Most importantly, it is in fact your responsibility to meet the business goals of the project, which are clearly being threatened if the project timeline is undermined.

There are some obstacles and delays, however, that simple focus and prioritization will not fix. Things like not getting FDA approval, or the design not passing test controls will put a serious dent in a timeline that might not be 'cure-able.' While you do not necessarily have to lead the group in assessing the damage and re-forecasting, you do have the responsibility to make sure this review happens and is communicated to the executive team. Not only does the project timeline need to be re-evaluated, but the entire project should receive some review to assess whether it is still viable and if any other parameters are impacted. A change to the FDA approval pathway, for instance, could dramatically affect the entire value proposition. One quick note: be careful that the delay truly is an 'incurable' one, and also look for any way that the negative can be turned into a positive. An example of this is when a product design fails testing and thus adds time to the schedule. You want to be sure to ask questions about the test parameters in order to understand why it was set where it was; you may find that the test 'breakpoint' means something other than it seems on the surface. Also, a design failure may indicate a weakness of a competitive device that can then be assessed and exploited. While this is not always true, be sure to ask questions and think ahead to see what you may be able to salvage.

Appendix

Because reimbursement can be a bit mysterious and scary (perhaps not for everyone, but for many product managers), the following two guides can help a bit.

The first is essentially the product development flowchart, but from a reimbursement point of view. What should happen within a reimbursement context during each stage? This outline plans it out. The only caution: this is a to-the-max reimbursement view and assumes that you have a full-scale need for reimbursement help. It *can* be scaled back for less intense situations.

The second resource is a guide on which experts are out there who can assist you with reimbursement/ healthcare economics questions/ concerns. In addition, there are a series of questions for you to consider asking that may or may not make sense based on your particular product/ need, but that at least give you some direction.

Reimbursement product development/ launch flowchart

Step 1:
On-boarding – Market Investigation
- » Get reimbursement expert involved right away
- » Assess existing codes and reimbursement amounts
- » Basic assumptions/ needs – intraoperative delivery means hospital and surgeon reimbursement, patient age xx% commercial insurance and xx% Medicare,
- » Outcomes assessed – most likely versus hi-low risk; obstacles and impact identified
- » Low/ no reimbursement issue should have surfaced by now – develop shortest timeline to validate issue and gather team to minimize risk/ pro-actively address

Step 2:
Validation – Development
- » Develop reimbursement/ healthcare economics action plan – studies needed, sites selected, linked with PMA study
- » Clinical affairs, reimbursement expert, and healthcare economist fully engaged and linked with marketing and development teams
- » Specialty societies, spokespeople, government influence action plans developed – will need to get to the "right people in the right places"
- » Start assessing PR value – possible PR outputs and venues
- » Channel assessment – not just sales, but also commercial insurance payers and hospital administration
- » Price and discount strategy developed and tested, along with messaging for all – surgeons, hospital administration, payers, and patients
- » Action steps and timeline drafted for reimbursement – who does what and when

PRODUCT DEVELOPMENT: MANAGING ISSUES AND MEETING DEADLINES

Step 3:
Commit – Manufacturing/ Build and Limited Release Launch
- Early studies underway and data collected assessed to prove/ disprove claims
- Discussions with CMS underway (following FDA approval) to gain new ICD-9 codes, may even get the new codes
- Discussions with specialty societies about CPT codes
- Active reviews of findings with team to develop publication strategy
- Reimbursement action plan gets underway – but it starts very slowly
- Who are your surgeon/ hospital advocates? Who will argue for this technology with commercial carriers?
- Prepare packets of information for the technology review committees

Step 4:
Full launch – Gaining Reimbursement
- This takes time! Happens one step, one commercial insurance carrier at a time.
- PR/ direct-to-patient campaign can help focus public demand
- Who is to be called with a problem? May need an appeals hotline, help desk for reimbursement issues
- Arm sales team with answers for possible questions

Reimbursement expert list and questions

REIMBURSEMENT EXPERT

- Is there a code/ procedure with which this would fit already? (At start, assume that there is not, that you will need a new code, and assume a new ICD-9 code that will also require a new DRG code. Payments must be higher, and you will need to use this to raise commercial insurance reimbursement and will likely need higher CPT payments for surgeons too. Work from hardest assumption to easiest, rather than assuming reimbursement is 'all good' only to find out it is not...)
- What information will be needed to establish a new code? Will we need to gather cost/ outcomes data during studies? (Remember, unlike FDA trials, CMS requires that you be able to extrapolate that information beyond controlled clinical trials to bigger population. In other words, you cannot have 'cream of the crop' patient selection criteria.)
- What information is needed to gain additional reimbursement so that the

price can be justifiably higher?   You will need to establish that there is a benefit for this; you must show improvement over existing options (or that there is no existing option).

- » Intra-operatively, you could focus on benefit over implants – natural tissue has improved performance/ function/ ligament connection/ etc, plus future ability to perform surgery, function of patient improvement, age of patient benefit – younger or older, less time in OR/ time under anesthesia/ side effects, etc.
- » Pre-operatively you could focus on alternative conservative treatments – NSAID's, watchful waiting, therapy, etc and possible negative impact that comes from reduced activity and pain
- » Post-operatively you could look at limitations that lead to cost – i. e., job changes, pain medications, continued therapy, etc.

CLINICAL AFFAIRS EXPERT

- Need to look at what studies can be designed that meet the needs outlined above
    - » Cost analysis – sites, focus areas, statistical analysis
    - » Population index – how do you extrapolate?
    - » What's the shortest timeline possible – short-term function studies that have peer-reviewed publication acceptance are critical
    - » Selecting sites/ criteria
    - » Control mechanisms
    - » How long will this take? How much will it cost?
    - » Will it delay time to market above the PMA approval? Can it be done simultaneous to PMA approval?

OTHER EXPERTS

- Make sure the regulatory and reimbursement expert link up over PMA study and includes questions in it that can benefit CMS/ commercial ins needs
- Bring in a healthcare economist to assess what additional studies/ information might be needed and include those costs/ timeline in your report

CHAPTER 4

Getting Product Launches Right

Launching products is not only a core competency of a product manager, but also one of the most fun and rewarding parts of the job…if done well. Putting a well-designed implant/ instrument system into the hands of the customer and knowing that you have been a part of really helping patients and making treatment/ life in the O.R. better just feels good. In addition, the sales team seems to just 'grab-n-go' when a strong product that is competitive, priced right, and positioned well is launched…and hitting those budget numbers feels good too!

All you have to do is…'just' get the product launched, along with all the necessary support tools to help the sales team in introducing it and demoing it to the surgeon and O.R. staff, shepherding it through the hospital purchasing/ stocking system, and in-servicing the O.R. team. Oh – and make sure that there is enough inventory on hand to supply demand, but not so much that the cost of carrying the system overruns profits…no problem, right?

Some of this ground has been covered to a degree in earlier sections; however, focusing on what is needed for a product launch to be competent and then what ingredients could be added to make it truly memorable is worth drilling into. Just like the adage 'practice makes perfect', or rather 'perfect practice makes perfect', a top-notch product launch takes a lot of behind-the-scenes sweat and 'practice' in order to pull off a well-orchestrated performance, especially one combining knowledge, precision, and creative flair.

Forecasting: putting the horse in front of the cart

Forecasting, along with building the numbers and checking/ re-checking them, is not generally fun. Not only do you know from the beginning that *whatever* you put down is wrong and that change is inevitable, but also you really need to start it so early in the process that you really do not know anything solid. This leaves the product manager wide open for criticism from all corners – why are we tooling up to build when you do not know for sure? Are we building enough? Are we building too much? Can the implant/ instrument set be scaled back? Should we break it into two or three sets? These are all questions you are likely to hear – *and should be able to answer as you get closer to launch*. However, the pressure is on to put together a forecast almost immediately, sometimes even before a project has officially begun in order to secure manufacturing space/ resources. And as soon as there is even a tentative forecast, there are sure to be questions as to how much, when, and why…and then, let the stone throwing begin…

So, how does a product manager handle this challenge and the questions along the way? This exercise/ question really translates into 'how can I modify the forecast for as long as possible?' and 'how do I make sure the right items are prioritized so the launch hits the ground running?' If you can satisfactorily take care of these two issues, then you have taken care of most of the forecasting issues inherent in product launches.

Forecast communication

Proactively setting up a forecast sub-team (if one doesn't already exist) can help tremendously. This should consist of the following roles.

(Note that the titles and division of responsibility vary among companies – assess what it looks like in yours. This group is generally three to five people.)

- Launch forecast owner (generally product manager, can have a sales management representative as well – this can be a different person than the forecast owner for a product that is already on the market.)
- Forecast/ production planner – can be two people if company has a forecast team and a separate manufacturing planning team, or can be one person
- Purchasing – could be combined with forecast/ production planner as long as that person has control over purchase orders and *actually does the follow-up*. The danger of not including the direct link to vendors, assuming vendors are a key aspect of the supply chain, is that slipping dates may seem minor or inconsequential to a purchasing agent, but one missed part could mess up assembly of a key instrument and then have an unexpectedly large cascade effect on time to market (or the next milestone).
- Engineering – Development/ Manufacturing – neither is a mandatory part of team, and they are not required once design is complete. Early

in the forecast cycle, it is nice to have some engagement, as issues of designability, vendors, and timing may very well raise their head during forecasting. This is truer at smaller companies than larger ones.

Once the team is in place, have a meeting as early in the business stage gate process as possible. The critical points of communication are:

- When would it be most helpful to have a preliminary forecast for planning purposes? Does it need to happen immediately or can it wait until farther into the design process?
- Define preliminary forecast predictability and timing…if one is needed immediately, then volume, set configuration, etc. will be highly volatile (no more than fifty percent accuracy); if later in the stage gate process, it will be more predictable.
- If possible, lay out game plan for forecast – when forecast updates are due and what level of accuracy is expected. This clears expectations so that everyone knows how much 'wiggle room' to leave in planning. Be clear on <u>when a final forecast is required to meet specific manufacturing dates</u> – you do not want to be the cause of missing release dates, and you also want to establish a sense of ownership and accountability across the entire company, starting with yourself.
- Talk about prioritization – when push comes to shove near the launch, what if there is the need to prioritize some implants/ instruments over others? How will that be handled?
- Discuss samples! They are a critical part of the launch in terms of market conditioning, prepping the sales team, and validating first waves of customer targets, yet they often get lost in the shuffle and thus pushed out to the end of manufacturing plans. You want the urgency of this on the table so that a make-buy decision can be made and samples are seen as a key aspect of the launch. 'Out-of-the-box' solutions (i.e., custom manufacturing, unusual vendor arrangements, etc.) may be alternatives if addressed early and prioritized.
- Other sets, i.e., loaners, workshops, and demonstration sets, may also need to be highlighted in order to ensure forecast is executed as you want it to be. This is especially true in some companies where sales demand is always prioritized over other forecast demand, and yet, during launch you want it handled differently.
- Make sure you know how U.S. versus international forecast and orders are handled. Sometimes the systems for forecast are different, and there is a difference in ordering that cause one to be accidentally prioritized over

the other. For instance, international 'forecasts' are automatically turned into 'orders' on their due date and then become backorder. Backorders take the highest system-wide priority and are filled/ shipped first. This may or may not match the true priority list.

Not all of this has to be addressed at the first meeting, although discussions about the initial forecast timeframe and expectations should definitely be addressed. This group needs to meet routinely throughout the project, and generally for three to six months post launch to track how set build/ release is progressing and whether the forecast needs to be adjusted up or down based on release and set turns.

Forecast methods

There is more than one way to 'skin a cat,' and your method should match the type of launch (line add, platform, etc.) planned. Things to take into consideration are: similarity to current systems, thoroughness/ effectiveness of your company's internal forecasting system, and confidence in the information/ targeting provided by the sales team. Because the product launch drives a tremendous inventory investment, developing a solid forecast that is both reasonable and defendable makes it much easier for the product manager to justify the expense. Additionally, while it is important not to forecast too much inventory, it is just as important (perhaps more so) to ensure there is enough inventory on hand to support sales growth.

Below are listed six methods of forecasting with a short description, along with benefits and limitations of each.

Method 1 – small number of sets released per month, forecast based on set turns

As sets are released, inventory is calculated based on expected number of surgeries per set for each month. There is a ramp-up time of one to three months as a set is released, with the uptake time due to getting the set into the hospital, training the O.R. staff, and getting cases scheduled. The ramp time can lessen if the sales force has more preparation (along with in-service support materials) prior to getting the set and can increase if the product is more innovative or costly.

During set 'ramp-up', general consensus is that fewer surgeries are booked until the set is established in the hospital and the O.R. team is comfortable/ knowledgeable with it. Since there is variability per set, the average 'ramp effect' is usually taken into account and then modified as launch occurs and real data becomes available.

Also, there is a difference of opinion on whether the turns/ set starts out high and decreases with the total number of sets in the field, or whether it starts out lower and increases as the total number of sets available grows. The start-high thought process is based on the theory that the initial targets are design surgeons and high-volume targets that typically do more surgeries than the 'average' surgeon. Thus turns decrease as more 'average' surgeons gain access to the product. With this concept, the general pattern is to see the average turns per set start high and then fall off for a short time before climbing up again.

The opposite low-to-high theory bases numbers on the thought process that the ramp-up effect mitigates the volume surgeon impact until enough sets are in the field. Additionally, surgeons may only switch a percentage of cases over to the new product, at least until they are comfortable with using it and with the outcomes. Thus, the net effect is that average turns per set starts out lower and then steadily ramps up over time.

Pros – relatively easy methodology to forecast once you have set the turns per set and per month multiplier and assessed how the 'ramp effect' will progress over time.

Cons – determining the turns per set is part science and part art, not something that is obvious. Without a prior product reference, good intelligence, and responsive/ lean manufacturing, there is a very human tendency to either under or over forecast – and either overstock (which kills profit) or undersupply (which kills the sales team with backorders).

Method 2 – small number of sets released per month, forecast based on field input

There are two ways to handle this method. One is highly individualized, in which each set is matched with the specific target and information gathered from the sales team in order to develop a very detailed forecast. The other method is to have the sales team by region or country (or whatever breakdown is used) put a forecast together of what they will sell, based on number of sets needed and/or allocated to them. This information can either be taken at face value or 'modified' up or down if the product manager believes accuracy is lacking.

Pros – The information can be tracked to either specific surgeon targets or to performance targets given by the sales team, which makes the forecast easy to explain and/or defend. Note that a high level of communication, trust, and accountability on both sides of the internal team (marketing/ manufacturing) and external team (sales) needs to exist for this method to be successful. Additionally, it is highly advisable for the sales team/ managers who are providing targets and forecasts to have extensive experience if you plan to go this route.

Cons – The target set-specific detailed forecast gets burdensome quickly. Additionally, while getting direct information from the sales team makes forecasting straightforward and defensible, it is likely that some data 'intervention' will be required in order to smooth the forecast and improve accuracy. When that happens, the 'easy' and 'explainable' benefit quickly gets lost.

Method 3 – larger 'batch' release of sets, forecast based on a similar product already available

In the situation that a large number of sets are released in intervals and when the product/ system is similar to another, then it becomes possible to build the forecast based on historical data. This can tremendously help in developing a solid forecast and even running multiple scenarios to assess how sets can be placed to max usage and minimize inventory. Analyzing the 'old' product(s) that the forecast is mimicking is important because variables impacting the launch that may not be reflected in historical existing data are identified and assessed.

Pros – In a large-scale launch, having a foundation to build from and being able to run predictive scenarios can really help in refining the forecast, as well as in explaining decisions. This is especially nice since the dollar amounts involved are generally quite high.

Cons – To work well, the historical product has to make sense as a predictor of how the new product will behave. This can be difficult since there are so many variables that may not line up exactly and could affect the predictability to some degree. Be careful in relying too much on the historical information without making 'tweaks.'

Method 4 – larger 'batch' release of sets, forecast based on set turns and/ or on sales team input

If there is not a historical product to use as a precedent, then it is still possible to work from turns/ set or information gathered from the sales team – or a combination of the two together. Even if forecasting from a precedent product, it may be worth doing a 'gut check' on turns/ set to make sure the forecast makes sense. One note, however, is that unlike with a smaller number of sets, it is highly unlikely that turns per set for a large number of sets will start high and decrease over time. Rather, it is much more likely that a significant percentage will take at least three to four months of ramp up time to fully engage and produce at expected value; thus, the more conservative approach is to forecast that turns per set will start lower and increase with time.

Pros – The straightforward method of turns/ set and/or data from the sales force makes the calculations relatively easy (once a spreadsheet template with assumptions on ramp and other variables has been developed). Categorizing sets into fast, medium, and slow ramp-up groups may increase complexity, but increase predictability.

Cons – The magnitude of an error is much greater because of the sheer number of sets involved. Without real thought and a careful breakdown of sets as calculations are made, over- or under-production of inventory will happen quickly. Think through the variables (like the speed of ramp-up) to see if adding two or three more variables could further refine the forecast. Consider regional variation of sizing for instance.

Method 5 – statistical forecasting during launch

With the right forecasting system and usually with the help of experienced analysts, statistical forecasting for launch can be a great tool. This is especially true for larger-scale launches and as a launch transitions from a few sets to more in the field. This process essentially combines the methods from above – data from historical systems, input from the sales team, input from marketing on expected uptake data, and any other variables accounted for. Additionally, the data can be broken down as finitely as desired - by country, region, or even distributor in order to more accurately predict need and track usage. It is a powerful tool if fully integrated into the company and readily available, although the product management team should take care to be in the loop, aware of the variables, and an integral part of the input and accuracy assessment. A quick 'gut check' from time-to-time to ensure the forecast plan simply makes sense on a basic level is a good idea – sometimes relying on a complex system can lead to overlooking the basics, plus it is likely that some things will need to be tweaked during the early phases.

Pros – This takes a lot of drudgery out of forecasting and allows focus on assessing the output and 'tweaking' based on field intelligence and assessment.

Cons – Without knowing how the calculations are made or the precedent the program pulls from, care should be taken to assess the forecast, especially in the initial phases, to make sure that it simply makes sense. Additionally, it is easy to become lax about staying involved in the forecast process because product managers aren't 'needed' any longer.

This is a mistake – while heavy-duty, every-day oversight is probably not needed, disengaging from forecasting altogether can cause a critical disconnect in information flow and decision-making.

Method 6 – quota system of set and budget assignment

There are companies that live (and die) by the business plan. Mistakes and mis-steps are simply not acceptable because the business is literally built from the ground up based on the plan itself. Sales team hiring and compensation, manufacturing overhead and capital expenditure, all internal budgets (including marketing) are based on hitting some percentage of organic growth, layered heavily with assumptions of sales driven by product launches. From a set placement and forecast perspective, the product manager and launch team has to be very careful about the plan put into place and coordinate its execution. However, once the plan has been accepted/ approved, much of the guesswork and even legwork from a forecasting perspective has been done. Sets are assigned based on some pre-determined factor (per the plan) – such as a territory's percentage of total sales, number of targets, sales growth dollar or percent, etc. Each set automatically carries with it a sales budget/ quota target that is assigned or added to the territory or region the set is placed in, often with some 'penalty stick' charge on inventory if the sales number is not met. Additional sets can be requested by a territory if they believe they can sell more, but they get an increased quota/ budget as a result as well.

Pro – Sales, inventory, and distribution are neatly packaged and accountability cleanly divided. This is a very logical system that makes forecasting a breeze - as long as the plan is put together and executed well.

Cons – If the sales team comes through with numbers and manufacturing/ set rollout happens as planned, there is really not one. However, if sales are less than planned, then watch out because the root cause will be found – and it will not be pretty. Blame abounds and in fact, tension tends to run pretty high in general in these types of companies. This can be a fairy-tale or a nightmare, so be careful.

Pricing – how much is too much? How much is enough?

STRATEGY

The first question that needs to be answered before determining price, or even how to go about deciding price, is what is the pricing strategy? There are actually two parts to this question:

a) What is the company's overall pricing strategy?
b) What is the product pricing plan, and does is alter over time?

In spite of the fact that price is supposed to reflect the market and that all of this should have been covered in the business plan phase of the project, there are typically minimum margin expectations that are required for an implant, and perhaps for instruments as well. While this is not technically a strategy, it can be a significant factor in setting price – or in developing a rationale for something different if required. Recognizing the hurdle is step one.

Some companies also have either a formal or informal price 'strategy' (or policy) that is codified around whether price premium or share growth is foremost. Additionally, there may be an overt or subtle differentiation in pricing between new 'technology' and new 'products', in which a new product that fills a market segment but is not a technological advancement is priced differently (lower) than an item that is deemed 'innovative'. Understanding how the company as a whole manages pricing challenges will simplify pricing decisions for a specific product, and relative standardization across the product spectrum can be beneficial to the sales team, keeping their pricing story consistent and raising competency in handling pricing questions.

The second part of the equation is the product pricing plan. This decision on where to price – premium, below the price leader, middle of the pack, or share-taker - needs to drive price point.

On the high end of the scale, a premium price point is fairly common when a product has technological advancements or clinical evidence. It is not uncommon to adopt a skimming policy to price high for a product (sometimes even one that is not 'hi-tech') when availability is limited and then reduce price/increase discounts as quantities increase. There are a few (usually large, market leader) companies that will price routinely at a premium or immediately below the published list price, but allow significant discounting to accommodate variation, essentially trying to hold both the high and low end of the price spectrum.

At the lower end, a share-taker price strategy is a sales-oriented approach to maximize the potential sales volume share gain post-launch by minimizing price as an obstacle. If the sales representative convinces the surgeon to try the new product, *not* having price as an obstacle in gaining access to the hospital is a huge time saver. However, simply having a lower price will not mean no discounts; thus, there will still need to be enough profit in the sales price so that discounts can be taken and still meet gross profit goals. Additionally, it is still important to make sure the sales representatives are adequately compensated and thus pull the new product out of their bag quickly and easily.

Making the price decision

Setting list price can be difficult, and it is up to the product manager to have a rationale for the decision. Some companies have guidelines on this, but many do not. Because of the questions on this subject, here are some 'rules of thumb' to consider:

Determining competitor list price and the range of typical discounts are critical pieces of information in accurately setting both list price and discount authority (at launch and later). Information gathered from the sales channel provides one source of information, but finding a second source via company price lists or third-party analysis/ research is much better.

In addition to that information, attributes of the product itself also should be taken into account. The technology and innovation of the device and the 'story' that goes with it is a great starting point. Some other things to take into consideration:

- Does the device have evidence (clinical/ scientific) to support a higher price in front of a purchasing committee? Will the product/ price have surgeon support and tools to answer the questions asked and justify additional expense? (Note: This is not 'general' justification, but specific, detailed analysis.)
- Does the sales channel have the capability to handle a price premium conversation and the issues/ challenges that go along with it? (Note that this is not a knock on sales channels, but rather a reminder to realistically assess the relative experience level, percentage of time dedicated to your product/ company, and whether there have been other products that have held a price premium. If not, then the difficulty increases exponentially.)
- Is the price premium worth the extra time that it takes to get through the purchasing and/or new technology committee and any other hospital delaying tactics? In other words, what is more valuable, the additional profit from a higher price or additional sales from higher volume?
- If going the price premium route, be prepared for questions about reimbursement. With a PMA product, this may be a question that you have prepared to answer by gathering information during the clinical trials. If so, you are all set, but if not, then you still need to prepare a response (with supporting analysis and sales tools/ materials).
- Many companies have intercompany transfer prices for international subsidiaries and for international distributors. In some companies, the

product manager is responsible for setting and managing these prices. Ideally, the company has some standard guidelines, but that is not always the case. A couple of questions to ask and concepts to keep in mind if you have to set transfer price and are not sure what to do are:

- » For internal subsidiaries, find out whether the more important factor for your company is see-through profit or transfer price gross profit. If it is see-through profit (in-market sales price less cost), then set transfer price based on cost plus some minimal percentage increase. If gross profit on transfer price is the critical factor (at least for you), first establish the minimum transfer price gross profit needed, usually around forty to fifty percent. Then, do enough due diligence to ensure that you set a transfer price with the highest margin possible, *but* one that still allows the subsidiary to get enough profit on the in-market price that it is worth their time and resource investment. It may require looking at procedure margin rather than individual devices to best assess how to set transfer price.
- » For international distributors, the only margin available is from transfer price/ sale; thus, the tendency is to set transfer pricing high such that profit is maximized for the company. However, at the same time, the distributor's profit is in-market price minus transfer price, and most distributors sell multiple product lines. Naturally, the distributor will favor products lines (and companies) that provide better profit for them. Also, distributors are generally expected to purchase initial inventory and instrument sets and need to generate cash to cover expenses. So, it is important to understand in-market sales channel and pricing well enough to set reasonable transfer prices with a solid margin for the company, yet still leave enough profit value so that it is a worthwhile product for the distributor to make an investment and to sell.
- » One note on setting transfer prices for re-usable/ non-disposable instruments – often these are priced for both subsidiaries and distributors to cover cost, with little to no corporate profit value. Make sure that there is enough of a pad that cost can increase on a couple of instruments and the transfer price will still adequately cover the cost of the entire instrument set. While you may be able to adjust the transfer price in some cases, it may be difficult to do so repeatedly.

One major pricing point is to ensure there is not an unresolved conflict between margin expectation and market forces/ dynamics. While this should surface well before this time (during business planning/ market research), there is a possibility that some issue has changed or that the product manager has come into the situation late in the game. If the product cost and margin required mean the price is out of line with the market, then launching a product that is priced wrong for the market is disastrous. Forcing the sales force to then deal with the consequences will not save the product and certainly will not help build a relationship with them for the future either.

Last but not least on pricing – remember the golden rule (on pricing that is): you can always go down, but you can never go up. Start higher and reduce or discount, but be very careful of advice to price low. Unless low cost/ high volume is your company's core competency, it is not a winning strategy.

Thinking about the field...

Price is an extremely important product attribute to the sales team, sometimes garnering more attention than seems reasonable. However, since the representatives are ultimately the face and voice (not to mention eyes and ears) of the company, it is a good idea to walk a bit in their shoes and see things from their perspective...

Two things will discourage a sales representative from pulling your product from their bag very quickly – 1) making less money than they do with comparable products (or alternatives they could sell), and 2) pricing the product so that it is not competitive in the marketplace.

In the first instance, the representative takes a look at what they have in their bag and also assess how he/ she is compensated on each item (taking into account both regular compensation and special promotions.) They then assess the time, effort, and difficulty associated with selling each product and figure out which is the most profitable route. So, if the representative is going to have to spend the same amount of time and effort and is paid less...or if he/she loses the opportunity for a higher-paying sale because of time spent doing grunge work on your product, then guess what? (Or wait...you probably already know...)

Note: Short side-bar for those who are making sarcastic comments in your head about 'money-grubbing' or other similar observations regarding sales representatives...you <u>want</u>, <u>need</u>, and in fact <u>hire</u> professional entrepreneurs who run their sales business to do exactly what your company does -- namely increase sales and maximize resources by utilizing the minimum amount of resources necessary (ethically and with integrity). The best sales representatives are great entrepreneurs and a peek inside of their heads as they calculate

ROI (return on their time/ product selection investment) is often a learning experience.

The second situation involves a non-competitive price, whether real or perceived. However, if the representative believes the product is priced out of the ballpark (and this almost always means too high), then he/ she may choose not to play ball. The first step in this circumstance should be a clear assessment on whether the representative is right or not (*not* whether you want the representative to be right or not). If the representative is *wrong*, then you need to address the perceptual issue regarding positioning, competitive strength, and training. However, if the representative is *right*, you can address wide variations in price requirements by setting up discount guidelines with approval controls at specific levels. Monitoring price and/or setting up a top-level price/ discount committee to review the highest discount requests provide for appropriate, discretionary discounts without dropping price overall.

EXAMPLE OF DISCOUNTING GUIDELINES:

Discount	Approval Authority	Information Required for Approval
0-4.9%	Sales Mgr	Complete discount documentation for pricing group.
5-14.9%	Distributor/ Territory Manager	Discount documentation, plus territory manager explanation on account specifics.
15-24.9%	Regional Director	All of the above, plus list of surgeons, products and expectation going forward - new business, retain account, etc?
25-34.9%	VP Sales	All of the above with business plan that shows ALL products in account and expectations going forward/ rationale.
35%-44.9%	Pricing Committee	All of the above, will also assess overall account profitability and business impact. Phone call with distributor/ regional director during committee discussion possible.
45%+	General Mgr/ Pres	All of the above, will require direct conversation regarding situation.
Pricing Committee Members:		VP Sales, VP Marketing, Director National Accts., VP Finance, Pricing Analyst

MEDICAL DEVICE MARKETING

Product and sales support

SALES COLLATERAL

Personal selling is the backbone of outreach to most physicians and healthcare/medical device customers. Distributors and sales representatives form long-term relationships with physicians and learn each customer's preferences both in surgery and in the office. They ensure that specialized needs and custom instruments are taken care of and are responsible for in-service training of the O.R. staff on implants and/or procedure-specific instruments. Because of the access and relationship between the sales representative, the physician/customer, and the O.R. staff, it often makes sense to develop specific sales collateral pieces that facilitate one-on-one conversations and convey technical information in an informal setting.

Listed below are typical sales support items with marks for what is included in a platform product launch versus a smaller product launch versus a line addition. However, every launch has to be customized for the specific needs of what the sales channel needs to go through: the steps of the sales process with each customer target. (Note: There could be more than one sales channel and/or more than one customer target, resulting in multiple sales funnel processes that need to be mapped and supported.)

Marketing Campaign/ Collateral - Items to Consider:	Platform Launch	Small/ Mid-size Launch	Line Addition
Basic Information:			
- Surgical technique	x	x	?
- Specification brochure	x	x	?
- Sales sheet(s)	x	x	x
- Animation	x	x	?
- Instructive PowerPoint	x	?	N
- List FAQ's	x	x	x
Hands-on Material			
- Clinical/ biomechanical data and white paper	x	?	N
- demonstration model and case	x	?	N
- Samples	x	x	?
Website			
- Site update	x	x	?

- Distributor portal update	x	x	x
Training - Surgeon/ Sales			
- Visiting surgeon program brochures	x	?	N
- Sales representative training program/ info	x	x	?
Advertising			
- Journal ads	x	?	N
- Patient education material	x	?	N
Public Relations			
- Press releases	x	x	?
- PR info/ pics for surgeon/ hospital mktg	x	?	N
Clinical Study			
- Protocol	x	?	N

While there are some foundational items that should be considered for every product launch (i.e., surgical technique), it is easy to get caught up in the 'more is better' syndrome and not really think through the 'why' of each piece of sales support. A practical (and generally much less costly) approach to developing a strong support package is to work with the sales team before and during the development and clinical/ limited release of the product to create a sales funnel specific to the product/ procedure.

The sales funnel is an idealized version of the process a sales representative will undergo, from introduction through conversion with the product. There should be between four and eight critical steps called out that every representative will go through during the process. Then a sales support piece or program is developed for each of these steps, such that each marketing support item in the sales representative's bag is intended for a specific purpose along the way toward converting a customer. This approach is intense in the beginning while developing the funnel and honing what support piece or program is best suited; however, once the decisions have been made, developing the items is much easier and extraneous pieces are eliminated. Additionally, the sales support package rollout with the product launch is precise and professional, designed for results.

MEDICAL DEVICE MARKETING

Example:

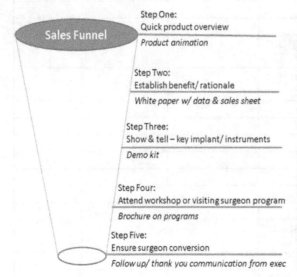

Sales Training

Because of the relatively higher intensity of training associated with a new procedure versus simply a new implant or line addition, training can vary from hands-on workshops to online learning modules and ongoing WebEx's. Typically, the earlier the sales representative is involved in the launch (i.e., with a design surgeon/ evaluator), the more training needed because the representatives are also early problem-solvers and can assist in developing the 'story' and sales funnel as a result. With more technical products and/or larger systems, training intensity and thoroughness need to increase. The representative must be prepared to in-service the O.R. staff and be confident that he/ she can handle problems/ issues that could arise in the O.R. without panicking.

Staging training to coincide with set rollout ensures that the training format is refined over time (assuming training sessions are evaluated and reviewed each time) and the representative does not forget information because the lapse between training and use is too long. Also, it allows knowledge to organically 'grow' as the more experienced representatives who have customers using the product can answer questions and on-the-job train. Some companies do not require representative training with a product launch; however, if at all possible, making training mandatory is a good idea. Not only does it ensure that the sales team is prepared, but also it brings a consistency to the message and story. As an additional argument for this requirement, more hospitals are now asking representatives or their companies to certify competency on specific products before allowing them into the O.R.

In some companies, sales training is a part of the product management function, while in others it is housed in sales or education. Regardless of the structure, during launch, product managers need to take an active role in planning and directing sales training. If other departments have the functional responsibility, then involve them in the process proactively early on and keep lines of communication open.

Physician/ Customer Education

In some situations, physicians will want to practice a new procedure before working on patients, especially before going into the O.R. Sometimes, even if the procedure/ treatment is similar, they may want to observe with another physician either because they are starting to use a new, unfamiliar system or they believe there are tips/ tricks that they can learn to improve outcomes.

The more formal training sessions include both cadaver and didactic sessions and are typically reserved for when a physician is learning something technically challenging. The less formal and more common type of customer training is via a physician visiting program in which physicians with experience and competence with a procedure/ system are selected as sites for other customers to visit. These are typically set up beforehand to facilitate the necessary paperwork for observation and to coordinate with the host both regarding schedule and the transfer of information. Alternatively, one-on-one cadaver sessions are sometimes held with a physician to allow him/her the opportunity to have hands-on experience prior to working with patients.

The product manager's role in this is first to assess if physician education is a critical path in the sales process and, if so, to provide for it. If it is not a typical step in sales conversion, then it may fall into the responsibility of medical education to handle these requests, although in some companies the product manager is still responsible. In either case, the product manager needs to ensure that the training and the message are consistent and meets expectations/ standards.

Market Studies

For products that incorporate technical innovation or for a system in which data (long-term outcomes or short-term studies) may be helpful, initiating clinical trials early on can be helpful. Note that the studies discussed here are post-market release studies, not required by the FDA or any other regulatory body for clearance or for surveillance.

There are two basic types of studies that can be put together. In the first, the surgeons validate the procedure/ system against another 'standard' procedure/ system in order to prove safety and effectiveness in multiple surgeons' hands in a variety of settings. This is essentially a defensive study in that the purpose is to prove the product (procedure/ system/ treatment) can be learned and used by a variety of surgeons successfully. The comparison chosen is something that is used widely and considered 'standard practice' across the industry. Thus, equivalency or favorable outcome demonstrates the new product is also viable across a wide market range.

The second type of study involves a series of data points on specific items to compare the newly launched product against competitors. In this type of study, the typical goal will be to show some benefit, such as reduced blood loss, less pain, fewer hospital days, greater efficiency, etc., that the new product (procedure/ system/ treatment) demonstrates versus the competition. (Note that 'competition' in this case can be a company, product, or an alternative treatment path.) When complete, it is hoped that the study results will show favorable performance benefits on key criteria that can be used to sway customer usage and/or cement current user loyalty. The risks are higher for this type of study because superiority is the end-point requirement; however, the reward is greater as well.

Additionally, data from these studies can be used for surgeon publications in peer-reviewed journals and podium presentations at scientific meetings. It can also be used to support white paper publications for sales representatives to leave behind as validation when presenting data to physicians about the benefits, value, and/or the safety and efficacy of the procedure/ system. If this path is followed, the information can also form the basis for the advertising campaign as well.

Scientific Data and Support

Sometimes running a market study either does not make sense or simply is not is not a feasible option. However, even when that occurs, a product launch of any size and depth still needs some consideration of scientific evidence in order to support the marketing story. However, if a differentiated position is planned, then the support requirements are significantly higher and must carefully interlock to make a compelling pathway for the customer to walk down.

While outcomes/ clinical data from multiple sites for demonstrating product superiority is ideal, it is very possible to construct a solid argument without it. Data from mechanical testing can be quite persuasive, especially if the same test can be run on competitive products to provide head-to-head comparisons. Also, material or chemical analysis from the lab can be very helpful. Again, if identical tests can also be run on competitor products, or if there is an industry standardized test for comparison, then the argument is strengthened considerably.

Theoretically, computer-generated data can be valuable, especially if it is in conjunction with other testing. However, even one stand-alone analysis can be beneficial and go a long way in driving a story home –if it clearly demonstrates the thought process/ analysis so that a non-engineer can understand it and is supported by easy-to-read pictures/ diagrams. Statistical data, either standing alone or drawn from meta-analysis, starts getting tough for sales representatives and customers to slog through, but again can be used effectively if it is either combined with stronger support or explained well with good pictures/ graphs.

One way to strengthen scientific data is to make it tangible – provide the sales team with a small, hands-on demonstration that illustrates the concept and makes it seem simple. Here is an example:

> All knee femoral components were made with complex multi-radius geometry, which was supposed to mimic natural bone and movement. One company decided to go a different path by stating that the natural bone was actually a single radius if looked at from the right perspective – and thus using their instruments/ tools to place the implant correctly, a single radius implant design was better. This is a rather complex concept and not something with clear scientific support. However, the company was able to clarify and support that differentiated position and claim market share, simply by having the sales team use a drinking cup or a can as part of their product demonstration during discussions.
>
> The sales representative would bring a cup or soda can with him/ her into the sales call. Then, during the single versus multi-radius conversation, he/ she would simply turn the cup or can on its side and show how a single radius (circle) rolls. Ideally, there would be some pencil holder or other oval-shaped container nearby (on the physician's desk) that the representative could then grab and 'roll' it to convincingly demonstrate the superiority of the singe radius concept, grabbing the physician's attention and answering a slew of 'scientific' questions with a quick (and most persuasively, hands-on) display. Best of all – this was before product ever made an appearance. What a great way to get a point across!

Another concept that can be effective if clinical data is either unavailable or not convincing is to purposely devise trials- usually in the lab- that test the limits of the product. While this will not make sense for every product/ system, it can be a powerful concept in talking to surgeons if the sales team can describe efforts to test the limits of the product and show that the company goes above and beyond the norm and the competition. The more 'out there' the test, the better, especially if the visual aids that go along with the test look good and are interesting. One big caution, however, is to make sure the engineering team is on board with this and work together to come up with solid protocols that demonstrate the product effectively, not demonstrate product failure. This type of thought process can be powerful for a new material (or new material usage), a new procedure/ indication, or for an instrument that will used in extreme circumstances.

Advertising/ communication plan

Advertising should fall from the overall launch strategy; articulating the product 'story' and highlighting any facts or data that support positive benefit conclusions. While advertising is typically thought of as only journal advertisements, other types of customer communication should also be considered and may be more effective for a specific purpose. The more important consideration in advertising is determining what message needs to reach a specific audience in a set timeframe. The communication need drives the advertising plan, which in turn leads to decisions regarding the advertising/ communication format used. The biggest mistake is to follow some prescribed plan without considering alternatives – spending money without knowing why or what results are expected is not acceptable, yet happens all the time.

Stages of advertising to consider are as follows, although note that variations exist and that this does not really address brand management on a larger scale. Thus, developing an advertising/ communication plan that incorporates elements of company/ product branding and positioning within a larger context will require more thought and analysis.

Specifically, the stages of advertising planning are as follows:

- Pre-launch conditioning – the focus of this communication is raising awareness within the market/ customer segment about an issue/ concern that is real, but may not be fully recognized or may simply be something that everyone lives with and thus about which no one is complaining. Ideally, a surgeon or other independent authority can be the source of information, or at least provide corroborating evidence, about the issue. Depending on the size of the concern, the underlying market understanding

of it, and the significance of the launch, pre-launch conditioning may focus on tradeshows and start three to six months prior to launch, or it may have an entire large-scale communication campaign that starts one year ahead of time.
- Launch – while communicating with the surgeon evaluators, early users, and sales team is always important, it may make sense to delay true launch advertising until enough inventory/ sets are available to satisfy demand. Once the time is right, the purpose of launch advertising is to pique interest and stake out market position. Generic advertising that is not memorable or does not have a clear point that is obvious by merely scanning the material misses the mark.
- Post-launch follow up – the story established and the data generated directs the campaign, although determining how the campaign helps with the sales funnel should be a critical aspect in shaping message and placement. If there is not a purpose and an expectation/ measurement of results, ask why you are spending the money.
- Other communication forums – several other means of larger-scale customer communication may provide more value than traditional advertising, depending on the message and the goal. Alternatively, a different customer segment may be targeted and thus lead to trying an alternative path.
  - » Direct mail/ e-mail – while lists can be bought, the trick is actually getting the right person to see and absorb the message. FedEx delivery helps on the 'snail mail' front in increasing the success rate of getting the material to the customer, but e-mail lists are hit-and-miss. While a well-targeted e-mail campaign with a short and sharp message or concept can be tremendous, the risk is that the e-mail address may have changed or be unmonitored/ monitored by an administrator. Is it worth the risk? it is your call.
  - » Sponsored media and/or other communication at a meeting – make sure it is both attention-getting and that there is a specific and compelling message.
  - » Self-selection campaigns via targeted websites – These are catching on as ways to reach interested individuals, especially in this increasingly digital age in which interested customers may very well search for information online and sign-up to find out more. It is a relatively new concept, but it may be worth exploring.

◀ MEDICAL DEVICE MARKETING

Public Relations

At the minimum, a press release announcing the product launch should be developed and communicated. Beyond the simple facts, this release should also contain the elements of the market 'story' the sales team will carry, bolstered by as many facts from studies or tests as reasonable. Timing the release for maximum impact (ie with a tradeshow or first surgery) makes it more memorable and newsworthy.

Taking it one step further involves developing a press release, pictures, and education kits for surgeons and hospitals to use in announcing and marketing the availability of a new product/ technology/ procedure in the market. Patient education materials may be considered as a part of this as well, although if a significant patient education campaign is undertaken, it should be a separate activity that is carefully planned and executed.

Public relations can also cover activities that impact the financial market. These can include such things as industry analyst sessions, interviews between physicians/ engineers/ executives with journalists, and summarizing the relative value of new products within the context of healthcare economic questions. Although the 'bent' of these conversations can be different than talking to a healthcare provider, it is still reasonable to have the key product message and benefits supported by data as an integral part of the statement to the financial community.

Web Site

Updating the web site to feature product information and post positive PR is a good way to keep communication flowing and generate positive conversation. Pictures, pre-launch publications, training opportunities, and any supporting data are all great additions. If a market conditioning plan was put into effect to highlight a specific issue/ concern that the product is addressing, then that information should also be featured both prior to launch as well as showcased in a solution-based forum afterward. Getting an early surgeon user to write up a case report with x-rays can be a great way to inspire confidence and increase momentum early in the launch, with more case studies showing additional indications/ uses added as the launch continues. There is even the ability to add a live surgery feed, either in its entirety or a clip, perhaps highlighting visiting surgeon sites.

Bottom line – the ideas are almost endless on ways to showcase the product on the web. The hardest part is settling on a few ideas and then following up to get information from the involved people so that early data/ input is available quickly. Nothing sells like success, and generating positive momentum early on can spur future sales.

Appendix

MARKETING AND PRODUCT LAUNCH PLAN

Below is an outline of a marketing/ product launch plan that you can use as a guide. There is no actual content, even in the section called 'attachments'. This is something for you to reference and cross-check as you are putting information together and to shoot for as a complete and well-rounded document. Note that it is <u>highly likely</u> that your particular product/ market will require you to change this up, hopefully to add some items and perhaps leave some things out.

Section 1: Overview of Plan
  I. Market description
   - Size
   - Customer segment(s)
   - Growth rate
   - Assumption list (highly important – make sure to note assumptions throughout the planning process. This not only helps if changed assumptions affect numbers, but also if someone disagrees with your financials, then you are able to back it up by more than just calculations.)
  II. Geographical segments
   - Markets under consideration – size and characteristics
   - Priorities – all at once or staged
  III. Target customers
   - Physician profiles
   - Other potential customers that may have an impact (OR, physician assistants, hospital staff, etc.)
  IV. Customer needs assessment
   - Description of user needs
   - Voice-of-customer inputs
  V. Value proposition
   - How the customer's needs are uniquely met?
   - Physician/ Healthcare provider, Patient, Hospital, Payer
  VI. Positioning statement
   - State the unique value within the market in light of the

competition in one to two sentences
- List 3-5 compelling messages to support position

VII. Strategic fit
- What specific strategy of the company does this address?
- How does this particular product plan fit/ grow/ develop this particular strategy?

VIII. Anticipated competitive response
- Who are the competitors most likely to react? (The ones most likely to be impacted are the ones to look at first.)
- What reaction? (i.e., based on last history, what will they do? For instance, a science-based competitor will attack based on testing, while a marketing-strong competitor will attack based on advertising/ positioning.

IX. Summary of key marketing tactics (from list in chapter above)

Section 2: Overview of Finances

I. Cost assumptions
- Instrumentation
- Implants
- Transfer cost

II. Pricing strategy
- Describe pricing assumptions and strategy
- Segment by geographical market
- Discount guidelines

III. Reimbursement (add details if issues exist, brief statement of facts if all okay)
- How will the product be reimbursed?
- How will the surgeon be reimbursed? The hospital?

IV. Summary of five-year revenue projections
- By major market
- Global roll-up
- Market share projections

V. Summary of sales execution plans
- By major market
- Instrument sets and set turns
- Twelve month sales projections
- Targeted customers/accounts
- Cannibalization
- Pull through

- Total roll up globally

Section 3: Overview of Marketing
   I. Sales training plan
      - Timing and format
      - Goals/ testing
      - Targeted personnel to train:
         » Sales management training
         » Sales representative training
         » Regional technical directors (if applicable) training
         » Ongoing representative training for new hires
   II. Medical education plan (for healthcare provider/ customer)
      - Geographical market/ regional breakdown (if applicable)
      - Company-sponsored education meetings
      - Society meetings/ tradeshows
      - Physician-to-physician site visit education
      - Physician/ customer VIP visit to company
   III. Marketing communications plan
      - Collateral material
      - Samples
      - Advertising schedule
      - Publication strategy
      - Direct to consumer/ patient plan
      - Practice enhancement
      - Presentations during physician/ customer visits
   IV. Sales messaging – How would you most effectively communicate the value proposition if you had:
      - One minute
      - Five minutes
      - Thirty to sixty minutes
   V. Risks/contingencies

Attached documents:
   I. Expense budget for launch
   II. Detailed sales execution plan (can be global or by geographical market)
   III. Tactical plan calendar detailing critical milestones to hit in twelve months post-launch
   IV. Project task list – what/when/who accountability

Go-to-market plan presentation format

As an additional help in making the product launch a success, the outline below for communication with the sales team in ensuring the necessary pieces are in place to both support the sales conversion/ sales funnel process and to manage it once the product has been launched. This presentation is intended as an interactive discussion with the sales management team as both marketing and sales come together in the final push prior to the actual launch. Goals for this meeting should be engaging and agreeing on the sales targeting strategy and key focus for conversion. Ideally, there is time set aside to draft and/or refine the thirty-second 'elevator' speech and to list three to five likely objections and responses.

Note that a draft version of actual slides has been included to help in visualizing how these might work in real-life. Also, and probably more importantly, slide eight shows a Sales Execution Worksheet that is intended to be developed with the sales management team. Marketing comes to the meeting with Slides 1-7 complete and a working draft of the worksheet (Slide 8) in order to facilitate discussion. This is a chance to think through what it is going to take to hit the sales budget number - and then plan and manage from the ground up. Thus, marketing and sales discuss how many potential prospects/ targets it will take to convert one customer – and then build from there to see what each territory/ sales team needs to do in order to over-achieve.

Following the meeting and building the sales worksheet, the product manager and a designated sales manager should meet together to develop a follow-up package with all the information and to what exactly each person/ group has committed themselves. Additionally, the product manager and sales management team should have some way to track and talk about how things are progressing – whether positive or negative – as the launch rolls out. The idea is to get real-time information and then adjust as quickly as possible based on what is learned.

Slide 1 – Market and Goals
Describe market (size/ growth) and the specific segment in which the new product belongs. What is our goal (market share capture, sales goal, sales per set)? In other words, why are we doing this, and how does it help us hit sales/ share goals?

Slide 2 – Value Proposition
Include basic value proposition and information on design team surgeons and/or other relevant data that supports your product positioning in the marketplace.

Slide 3 – Competitive Targets
Who are we going after to gain new business (no more than two to three targets)? Why are these targeted systems/ competitive users?

Slide 4 – Product Benefits/ Key Drivers
What makes our system 'the best' (or substitute whatever messaging/ positioning statement you are looking to drive)? How are we better than the competition? This will need to be focused on the main drivers, as not everything can be listed.

Slide 5 – Training Plan
Who gets trained, when, and how? Is training required or merely a nice-to-have? Who communicates training mandates (if applicable), testing, etc.? Who holds accountability? How will training be conducted – site visits, WebEx, online module, etc.?

Slide 6 – Sales Support Plan
This includes samples, literature, competitive comparison, digital, etc. NOTE that this should be matched to a sales funnel/ conversion process. If it is not, now is the time to think about it. Draft one along with a script, use the sales managers and engage if you have not done it before.

Slide 7 – Actual Rollout Timing
This is the number of sets and when they are going out? This is also the tie-in to the Sales Execution part – the sales management team can partner with marketing in assessing the conversion rate, the ideal prospect/ target, and determine how sets should be prioritized during rollout.

Note that additional slides can be added to suit content, and, in fact, there are more than seven slides in the example below. The important aspect is this: *mutual accountability*. Your goal is to walk away with the sales team holding you accountable for certain deliverables <u>and</u> you holding them accountable for certain deliverables. Just as important: both groups need to know and agree on for what they are accountable and how they will assess/ communicate as the launch actually happens.

Slide 1

PRODUCT NAME
Marketing & Sales Execution Plan
for 20xx

MM/DD/YY

Slide 2

Strategic Overview

- How does this product fit into XYZ's new strategy of growing the --- market?

(Will likely be one of the 3 listed below)
- Is this product line complementary to that strategy?
- Core to strategy?
- Necessary for some other reason?

Slide 3

Market & Goals

- Short positioning statement and 20xx goals (ie grow 2x market rate and target Competitor A's product)

MARKET
- Market Segment:
- Market Size:
- Market Growth:

GOALS

	2010	2011
Market Share:	x%	x%
Sales Goals:	$xxM (% growth)	$xxM (% growth)
Sales/set:	$xxk / set (# sets)	$xxk / set (# sets)

Slide 4

Value Proposition

- What are the key points of the 'story'?
    - Main drivers?
    - Why is this better?
    - Why can sales reps win with it?

- What is our focus to drive growth (or reach goals) for 20xx?
    - Example -emphasize clinical results with white papers
    - Example -have key designers present at med ed meetings

Slide 5

Competitive Targets
Main competitors for focus on 20xx- this is who to take share from...in priority order

Company
- Product name (short descrip)
- Key attack point – how do we win?
- Key issue – what are we concerned about?

Company
- Product name (short descrip)
- Key attack point – how do we win?
- Key issue – what are we concerned about?

Company
- Product name (short descrip)
- Key attack point – how do we win?
- Key issue – what are we concerned about?

Slide 6

Targeting and Segmenting: Profile the Ideal Account

- What is the ideal account that the sales force should go after?
    - Surgeon profile
    - Account size/ volume
    - Competitor usage
    - Other factors?

Slide 7

Requirements for Execution

NOTE – very important: *This slide is for you to note any specific needs to achieve plan – this should be above and beyond the current 20xx marketing plan. Add categories if required.*

Sales Force Needs – samples, add'l support, etc.

Sales Force Training – timeframe, testing, faculty, etc.

Surgeon Education – if needed

Set Deployment/ New Sets Needed – by region, by customer, etc.

Samples/Workshops/ Conventions/ Display – when it will be shown, how to make a splash, how to support the launch

Sales Literature – including digital media

Slide 8

Sales Execution Worksheet

PRODUCT NAME	2009 (act)	2010 (est)	2011 (plan)
Market Size			
Market Growth	NOTE: This is a planning worksheet to allow marketing and sales to estimate the # of potential customers that need to be targeted and filling the sales funnel in order to meet sales goals.		
% Market Share			
ASP	1000	1100	1200
Procedures/ Set/ Period (Turns)	3	3	3
Incremental Sets		100	100
# Sets	100	200	300
Gross Sales	$3,600,000	$7,920,000	$10,800,000
Growth Rate		120%	36%
Cannibalization Rate	1%	2%	3%
Cannibalized Sales	$36,000	$158,400	$324,000
Net Sales	$3,564,000	$7,761,600	$10,476,000
Sales per Period	$297,000	$646,800	$873,000
Procedures per Period	297	588	728
Procedures per Surgeon per Period		2.0	2.2
Surgeons Required		294	331
Incremental Surgeons			37
Conversion Rate %			50%
Targets Required			73
Targets by DM/TM			2
Conversion by DM/TM			1

Slide 9

What if...we needed add'l 10% sales?

- What actions could we take?
- What investment would that require?
- How confident are you that this would work?

NOTE: This is an exercise to develop alternatives that may be needed to boost sales. However, it is *extremely important* to acknowledge that additional resources of $$, time, people, etc. will be required in order to meet higher sales. DO NOT separate the numbers from the resources at any time.

Worksheet from Slide 8

PRODUCT NAME

		2009 (act)	2010 (est)	2011 (plan)	NOTES
1	Market Size				Fill in as background & as sanity check against #'s below.
2	Market Growth				
3	% Market Share				
4	ASP	1000	1100	1200	Fill in info based on business plan.
5	Procedures/ Set/ Period (Turns)	3	3	3	
6	Incremental Sets		100	100	
7	# Sets	100	200	300	
8	Gross Sales	$3,600,000	$7,920,000	$10,800,000	
9	Growth Rate		120%	36%	
10	Cannibalization Rate	1%	2%	3%	Bus plan - adjust as needed
11	Cannibalized Sales	$36,000	$158,400	$324,000	
12	Net Sales	$3,564,000	$7,761,600	$10,476,000	
13	Sales per Month	$297,000	$646,800	$873,000	
14	Procedures per Month	297	588	728	Sales divided by ASP
15	Procedures per Surgeon per Month		2.0	2.2	Estimate & adjust
16	Surgeons Required		294	331	Procedures per month divided by surgeons per month estimate
17	Incremental Surgeons			37	
18	Conversion Rate %			50%	Estimate & adjust
19	Targets Required			73	Incremental surgeons divided by conversion rate
20	Targets by DM/TM			2	Targets required divided by Districts/ Territoritories
21	Conversion by DM/TM			1	Incremental surgeons divided by Districts/ Territories

CHAPTER 5

Managing an Existing Product Line, Successfully

While launching a new product is fun and exciting, the important day-to-day work of a product manager is managing existing products. The ability to successfully direct a product through its lifecycle is the mark of deep expertise. Additionally, an expert product manager has the skills to assess a product's status within the competitor and technological market framework. The purpose of this assessment is not only to maximize offensive and defensive messaging/ positioning, but also to determine profitable line additions or system upgrades that may extend life and improve sales.

It is very common for a product manager to 'assume' responsibility for a product/ system at virtually any point in the lifecycle. While ideal to be involved with a product through the entire development process in order to have deep conceptual and technical understanding of it, a product manager can use the 'taking over' event to perform an external (field-based) and internal (engineer-based) analysis of the system in order to find both opportunities and inconsistencies. This can lead to an even better perspective of where sales or profit dollars can be found in order to meet goals.

Connecting to the sales team... getting them on your side, or rather, selling your product

A nearly universal truth that is generally acknowledged is sales representatives choose what product they will pull out of their bag first and definitely have 'favorites' of which they sell more. Another 'truth' that is less acknowledged, although recognized via quotas and sometimes promotions, is that sales representatives often do not have enough time to sell every product in their bag to its fullest potential; thus, there is a correlation between how much a sales representative likes a product and sales volume/ growth. This essentially means that the battle for a representative's heart and mind is a battle for sales.

So, what does that mean for a product manager? It should mean a lot because it opens up clear routes for the product manager to directly influence sales via engagement and interaction with the sales team. Just as the product manager must 'fight' for the priority and internal resourcing needed, a strong product manager will 'fight' for share of heart and mind with the sales team.

Methods to win hearts and minds

How specifically can a product manager engage the sales team? What about re-engaging a sales team that is not fully committed to a product line? Below are some specific suggestions and ideas, along with questions and thoughts on when each might be appropriate:

- Communicate, communicate, communicate – if the sales team does not know who you are or how to get in touch with you, they will struggle to have the confidence in pulling the product out of the bag, especially if they perceive technical issues or possible pitfalls. However, if the field knows you, and you put out relevant information *on a routine basis*, it makes the product a lot easier to grab with confidence.

When is communication to the sales team something to step up?

» If you are new to the company or new to the product, communication is key to get the sales team to connect you to the product. It is also important for representatives to know how to get in touch with you.

» If there is a constant state of emergency or steady stream of questions regarding one issue (or even a handful of them), then it is time to take a 'time-out' from being fire marshal and address the root issue. Do not expect the communication to 'fix' the problem – it will not... the sales team will still call even after the field information has been sent out. So, what is the purpose? Having an answer prepped and ready to send out means that you can be responsive to calls, e-mails, and messages on a personal level *without having to spend time*. That builds trust and creditability (see section below) with minimal effort... great opportunity.

» If there is a recall or some significant event within the product's life, *especially if it is negative*, then communicating with the sales team appropriate information on a timely basis is critical to gaining trust as a product manager. Going a step beyond with personal communication (meaning phone call, not e-mail) to those in the sales

- Be real and truthful about what is going on. This means addressing what is holding back the sales team from selling. It is fairly common for there to be two to five underlying core issues that have been ignored or mishandled in some way, often because it is costly or acknowledges some kind of weakness/ flaw in the system and there is not an easy fix. Sometimes one or more of these 'issues' have been attributed via 'common wisdom' to lack of sales force training or customers not using the product properly. Do not accept 'common wisdom' as truth without a thorough investigation. The sales team may grumble and fuss, not believing your efforts. However, persistence and honesty, combined with action (fixing an instrument, gathering data, putting together a study, etc.) will make an impact.

What to do if you do not know the issues?

» Well, the first thing to do is find out what is going on by talking to anyone who has experience and history with the product – engineers who were on the design team, sales representatives who sell or have sold the product, other marketing team members. Generally speaking, finding out problems is not difficult – most everyone is willing to share complaints or problems.

» Part two is harder – find those people who either have developed 'stories' that overcome the issues or have ideas on what would (short of an entire product re-design). Typically, these can be internal people who are 'closers' often asked to assist the field in finalizing a customer conversion with this particular product. Alternatively, there may be some representatives who have developed ways that they pitch the product to overcome objections, or at least some of them; often these are people who are selling now or who have sold significant amounts in the past. Often there are also engineers or other marketing people who have ideas about testing and/or synthesizing data (internal or published) that can be put together. (Note: Sometimes the most vocal critics end up with the most/ best ideas. Do not get bogged down, but do not avoid them either.)

» Observing the customer using the product to validate reported issues, especially if you can also see competitive systems that are reportedly better, can be extremely helpful. Not only can this confirm other sources of info, but also it can narrow focus and prioritize possible responses. Sometimes what appears to be the biggest issue really is not. Instead, it is the one that has the most 'shock value' and thus gets sales force attention. With no one speaking out to address any of the issues, it becomes the poster child symbol but is not really an underlying core problem.

- Recognize that money does talk – and that time is also money. If the sales team makes less money on a product or if they have to spend more time on it routinely, then they will view it as a lower 'profit' item on their business scale. If you think of sales representatives as entrepreneurs who are looking to maximize return, it can impact how you price, set up discount/ commission structure, bundle add-in/ disposables, or even look at the relative time and effort based on number of instrument trays. A product manager that *only* talks about dollars or assumes that it is the only representative driver will miss the bigger picture, but assessing fairly your product cost/ benefit versus others may lead to some surprising information.

PERSONAL CONNECTION TO THE SALES TEAM

First, before addressing any other item, the issue of product manager creditability needs to at least be acknowledged. For some of the ideas below to work, the sales team must believe and trust in the product manager as an expert resource and someone that they can count on to provide them answers, as well as be an asset in front of their customers. This kind of creditability is earned one step at a time by actually <u>being</u> a resource and by <u>listening</u> and <u>responding</u> to the sales team. Early on in a product manager's career or time in a new position, care must be taken to prep for every sales representative/ surgeon meeting with professionalism but not to pretend to have answers or information when you do not.

Along the same lines as creditability, the presence and 'likeability' of the product manager plays a role in gaining sales team heart and mind. If the field knows who the product manager is and likes him/ her, the personal connection significantly helps in adding weight and value to every other communication that the product manager does. This is essentially being part of the team – there is no way to be part of a team if the rest of the team does not know anything about the product manager, or feels like the product manager fumbles/ ducks/ runs when a tough issue or question comes his/ her way. Be in the trenches with them.

While some people find getting to know the sales team a natural extension of their personality, others are not naturally as extroverted and thus may need to deliberately get their 'name' into the field. One way to increase field presence is to take any opportunity to socially interact and get to know sales representatives on a more personal level. While these conversations may be entirely social in nature, it is not uncommon for the sales team to use these opportunities to talk about 'what is really going on,' which can be very useful for further information gathering, for addressing an issue, or for correcting misinformation. (The product manager role has an element of host/ hostess in it – participating in social events is in fact part of the job.)

When dealing with a large sales team, it is not always possible to know everyone. But there are always, always representatives and/or distributors who form an inside 'gossip' network. (This is true of both large and small sales teams.) With larger sales forces, there can even be a couple of critical networks, often comprised of the 'legacy' guys who have been with the company for a longer period of time (ten or more years) and the 'younger' guys who may have been with the company for a while but are recent additions to the sales manager team or who have more recently joined the company. Although these groups can be more difficult to crack, figuring out who some of these key players are and getting to know a few can be a great way to increase creditability, gain knowledge, and become known.

Another way to develop field presence is simply to spend time in the field. There is, however, a bit of trick involved in that a sales representative is uncomfortable having an unknown, untested product manager in front of their valuable customers, which frankly puts business at risk if the product manager messes up. There are a couple of ways to approach this:

1. Some distributors/ representatives like teaching and will take product managers to observe surgery and to visit customers with whom they have a strong relationship, with the understanding that the calls are for learning purposes.
2. Go on 'ride-alongs' to visit non-customers with product objections, in other words non-risky sales visits because the representative is not getting anywhere anyway.
3. Visit surgeon consultants to observe surgery and/or talk about a project, publication, or study. (Again, lower risk because these are customers with an already existing business partnership in the form of a consultancy or other type of contract. Thus, there is typically an active project and internal relationship in place.)
4. Set up a sales training road show that involves presenting to a distributor's

sales team.

NOTE: Although not always detailed, a product manager's job includes taking on a host/ hostess role at meetings and in social situations in working with customers and the sales team. This allows for more informal information gathering and communication that is critical, although it means that essentially there is little true 'personal time' for a product manager while at a meeting, convention, or company event.

New is always better…is it not?

Managing a product line through the beginning phases is fun (generally) when the sales team wants the product and wants you (most of the time). However, as the new glow begins to fade, the reality of competitors who can meet or even beat aspects of the system start setting in, and that is when the true work of a product manager has just begun. Just to clarify…this is not talking about the lumps, bumps, and bruises suffered during the post-launch/ early adopter phase when a few things surface that need to be fixed and the competition starts taking potshots. That is just part of the growth curve leading into the maturity phase and needs to simply be handled one at a time, with thoughtfulness, in order to keep momentum moving forward for as long as possible.

(NOTE: However, it is during this growth phase that unresolved issues/ objections can leach the life out of a product and keep it from ever reaching potential. It is also these same issues that may well be uncovered when a new, incoming product manager investigates the root causes of lagging sales and finds that problems were never addressed during the post-launch phase.)

The issues in this section relate to a product that has been on the market long enough to be fairly well-established. Because there can be so much variation in the length of time within a product lifecycle, depending on both the industry and the product, below are some criteria that a 'mature' product exhibits:

- Implant/ instrument supply is readily available and new customers can be accommodated quickly, even if that means via a loaner set while a new set is built. Launch sets (per the launch forecast) are no longer going out the door.
- Inventory on the market and in the field are all final versions, not prototypes or non-standard.
- Majority of the sales team (seventy percent or more) is comfortable with the product and can speak knowledgeably about it, including doing a workshop or demonstration.

- Sales support material, including samples and workshops/ demonstration kits, are easily obtained by the sales team to use during sales calls. Most sales representatives either have their own or have easy access to written sales support material.

As the product stabilizes, the product manager breathes a sigh of relief. But that sigh can quickly turn to concern as growth flattens and the sales team's attention shifts to shinier, newer products. What to do now?

Analyzing an existing product line

The strategic foundation has been laid, the messaging/ branding established, and the product position communicated. So, unless there has been a radical shift in the marketplace, what is there to analyze within an existing product frame?

First, just as the sand at the beach shifts in small increments and yet the entire shoreline can change shape overnight, the competition makes moves that shift the market dynamic. Some of these changes directly challenge your product; others indirectly impact simply because they raise an issue within the marketplace that was not even considered previously. These competitive actions/ reactions change the way customers think and shape conversations in a different direction, virtually overnight. An example of this happened when Zimmer started talking about the 'gender knee':

> Zimmer engineered a knee femoral component that was designed specifically for the dimensions of the female bony anatomy of the knee joint. While every knee system had validated proportional sizing to cover a range of male *and* female knees, no one had specifically called out one gender as having unique proportions that their implant was ideally suited to cover. Zimmer further changed the market dynamic by moving quickly to a direct-to-patient campaign that caused conversations between patient and doctor to shift. Thus, every company and every sales representative suddenly had to defend their knee for use in women. Additionally, many surgeons were looking for assistance in handling patients' questions when they used non-Zimmer knees. Not only did the entire market change, but also new physician and patient demands became part of the equation, very quickly and unexpectedly. In other words, Zimmer shifted the market dynamic – now virtually every company addresses the issue of 'gender knees' in some form or fashion (although no one can claim the first mover spot that Zimmer captured.)

Secondly, depending on the company, analysis of the sales channel situation may be in order. Differences in the quality, depth, and exclusivity of the channel can dramatically impact whether the strategy, messaging, and positioning are in fact clear and make sense. Additionally, if the sales team has either had a high turnover rate or a high growth rate, then the knowledge base may be lower than believed. Assessing the sales channel's comfort and knowledge with a product is a good way to check the foundations of positioning, support and training to make sure they have stood up to the test of time.

Third, during the launch, careful planning to match sales support material to the sales funnel should take place in order to maximize value and improve sales team efficiency/ effectiveness. However, after the product has been on the market for a while, it is highly likely that the sales funnel has evolved, perhaps even become multiple funnels based on specific customer segments. This indicates a greater level of sophistication as the representatives become more familiar with customer types and develop an understanding of how to best achieve conversion. Re-charting the sales funnel(s) and then evaluating sales support, including all support programs and mechanisms, can reveal both over and under-spending, allowing the product manager to make wiser budget decisions with scarce resources. It may also reveal that there are added market segments and customer profiles than originally targeted during launch, which may open new doors to product add-ons or sales support ideas.

Finally, there are the ongoing decisions to add products – instruments or implants – to the system that should be assessed. When these are for a specific customer or customer group, it is a relatively straightforward financial analysis. However, when it involves a more complex scenario regarding inventory and cannibalization and customer retention/ capture, then the question of whether to update a product line starts getting sticky. Also, it is possible that as the market shifts and the product grows; new customer segments with different profiles may emerge. This is especially true if the company is small and climbing the growth curve, or if the product has been introduced into new markets that have not been explored yet.

To update or not? – That is the question

There is a tug toward updating an existing system in order to meet customer preferences, but there is also an equal pull to launch new product platforms that are innovative and will 'build' on a previous system. Where should the line be drawn to stop adding to an existing system and build something new? Or perhaps the question could be phrased "How much updating is too much before it overburdens an 'old' system and makes the system appear to be on life support?

How to justify

From a financial perspective, the product manager has a much easier time building a business case for a new system when the inputs are clean and the outputs are always new sales less cannibalization. Typically, assumptions regarding sales growth (based on either number of sets and turns or on 'riding' market growth trends) are made in order to come up with future sales estimates. Alternatively, justifying line additions to an 'old' system is much harder because sales already exist and pointing to a single line addition/ upgrade within the product as a driver for significant incremental sales is rarely possible. Rather, the line additions or upgrade is more often contemplated in order to continue sales growth or even to prevent sales loss. The counter-question of 'what would sales be if we did nothing' is quite challenging to answer, particularly since the only real way to gather data on either side of the argument is actually doing it. Also, often the 'stand still' sales assumption is the budget, which may be too high based on the erroneous assumption that the product will grow without intervention. The line addition might be needed just to make budget, but the expense was not planned...now what? Thus, it is most often up to the product manager to make the assessment and then to make a convincing argument on why money should be invested in product upgrades.

Options to consider

When product additions/ upgrades are requested, there are three basic decisions that the product manager can make:

1) Decide not to pursue at all –

   This is usually because the request can be satisfied with some other instrument/ implant, because the request is more of a complaint than a requirement, or because the request falls outside the company's clear prioritization plan.

   (NOTE: it is very rare for a company's priorities to be so clean and clear that a request is really turned down based on not meeting criteria.)

2) Decide to handle on a 'custom' basis –

   This is usually because the request is limited in nature to one or only a small group of customers and not believed to be a business driver.

   Alternatively, if in doubt that greater resource expenditure is worthwhile, but there is still the need to satisfy a particular customer, then the 'custom' option can be used as a test market option by simply making one or two extra and shipping it around to select sites to gather feedback needed to build a business case.

3) Decide to put together a business case –
This is indicated when it is believed that the parts requested (instruments, implants, or both) are required to drive business. Ideally, the business case outlines how the upgrade provides one of the following:

- access to a different customer group
- cements conversions in a greater percentage of current target customers
- increases indications or increases number of cases that a surgeons will do with the system (because it either makes it easier to use or allows it to be used in more types of cases)

Alternatively, there can be a business case based on keeping sales or slowing the loss of sales. This can be based on one of the following:

- matches competitor system offering, allowing surgeon to effectively treat same patient range as the competition and thus takes away benefit of converting to 'their' system
- allows surgeon(s) using current product/ system to justify continued use in the face of competitive threats, generally balancing the scales such that comfort with current system outweighs some new competitor offering
- fixes problem with system, whether real or perceived, as experienced by a group of surgeons; this typically involves a subgroup of surgeons with similar training or background who have some issue that does not go away regardless of the explanation or technical intervention.

Note that not every business case results in a go-forward decision; thus, some of those 'no-go' decisions will result in going back to scenarios number one or number two above. Even in those cases, communication is still key; any physicians or customers affected need to know the outcome/ plan at a summary or overview level.

A BALANCING ACT

Ultimately, the decision to put together a business case and 'pitch' for resources has to be a balancing act. There are always requests for additions and upgrades, and a ton of these requests will come with 'justification' to make it a full-scale line extension as opposed to a custom, one-off response. However, there are very real limits to what can be developed, tested, and manufactured. Making promises that cannot be kept on a timely basis is not the right thing to do, and neither is tying up resources on a laundry list of items so that big-ticket projects are slow and cumbersome.

When the product manager decides to put together a business case, he/she also has a responsibility to fully assess and reveal positive and negative factors that may impact the project. These are *particularly* important factors that may not be self-evident, such as when two projects appear equal but one is likely to move faster because of *xyz* factors. Thus, the product manager has to decide where to best place his/ her influence to get results. While an understanding and instinct develops as to which projects to investigate, below are criteria to consider when sifting through business plans, particularly when numerous potential projects appear to be roughly equal on the surface or when the product manager wants some additional validation/ verification of assessments.

Assuming rough equivalence in return on multiple projects, below are some questions/ considerations to work through in developing a priority matrix, with the ultimate goal of the product manager having a clear view of which project(s) should be the highest priority:

- Time to launch: the sooner, the better – is it really that simple?

    The size and scope of the project impacts both actual time and risk factors that can delay launch. Instruments are faster than implants, and fewer are always better. Anything that requires testing and/or regulatory filing (versus a letter to file on an existing 510k) adds time and the risk of delay. It also indicates that some kind of clinical testing and/or limited launch is likely needed before full launch, which is resource and time consuming. Time requirements for instrument trays, if needed, and manufacturing can also significantly impact time to market. Each of these factors can raise complexity, resource-use, and add time. The fewer factors involved, the simpler and less risky the project.

- Past history is a good predictor of future success – who is really likely to sell?

    While information on some projects are gathered over time from a variety of sources, it is fairly common to have some group of the sales team and/ or country who are highly interested in a specific project claim that they can deliver sales results if said project is completed. This data is often used in support of a business case, and even if the data is carefully analyzed and assessed, it still comes down to some level of belief that sales will, in fact, result. So, in looking at competing projects, one aspect to compare is who has delivered on promises of sales in the past. Those people, and thus those projects, generally have a higher probability of reaching the success criteria simply because past success is a good predictor of future success.

- Past competence makes everything faster – has it been done before?

    If it has been done before, and if the folks at the company have a comfort level with the product(s), then there is less 'finagling' that has to be done and everything moves slicker. What is 'finagling' exactly? Well, it can be developing the computer programs to run manufacturing machines, creating quality inspection procedures, finding good vendors to outsource, or any number of other things. But, something that looks simple and easy may or may not really be; however, if the people you work with really *know* what it takes to get it done, then they do not have to guess.

- Too many cooks in the kitchen …is it going to take a lot of people?

    If parts have to go to multiple vendors or there are numerous groups that have to work together to make the project happen, the number of places where misunderstandings can occur and things can go wrong multiply. This can push out the launch schedule, but it also can mean that the project itself gets a bit lost and morphs during the process. In either case, the end may not reflect what is expected at the beginning, and those who were enthusiastic at the start may or may not feel the same at completion. If it is a tortuous path with lots of touches/ changes along the way, it is not going to be slick and quick.

Appendix

Marketing plan sample

Below is a sample/ outline of a marketing plan that can be used to put together the business overview for an existing product line. There may be many other factors/ areas to consider that are specific to your product area/ market, but this should get you started and cover the fundamentals.

MARKETING PLAN OUTLINE

I. **INTRODUCTION**
Define the product and describe the market in which it competes. Provide a brief history of the brand, including dates of entry of forms, sizes, and a history of market share.

II. **EXECUTIVE SUMMARY**
Provide a concise synopsis of the entire plan which focuses on situation analysis, strategies, and tactics employed.

III. **BODY OF PLAN**
Detail the what, when, where, how, and why

  I. <u>SITUATION</u> - Analyze the current market place for the product and set up the premise for strategies and tactics which follow.
  A. Market overview – Use three to five years of relevant data
   1. Market growth
   2. Market/customer segments – e.g., physician, hospital, pharmacy, managed care, government, nursing home, etc.
   3. Pricing situation
   4. Competitive products and shares
   5. Profile of physician, patient usage
   6. Key decision makers - physician, nurse, patient, payer, other
  B. Competitive activity
   1. Major brands, strategies and positioning
   2. Spending – amount and type
   3. Distribution
   4. Competitive strengths and weaknesses

  II. <u>KEY ISSUES/PROBLEMS/OPPORTUNITIES</u> – Discuss key issues and problems facing the product. Speculate on the future - - e.g., changes in government regulations, healthcare market, business climate, new competitors, line extensions, company resources, etc.
  A. Problems and opportunities
  B. Marketplace attitudes
  C. Trends
  D. Distribution
  E. New competitors
  F. Medical/regulatory/legal changes

MEDICAL DEVICE MARKETING

      G. Manufacturing and logistical problems
      H. Changing customer needs
      I. Geographical issues
      J. Manpower issues

III. <u>OBJECTIVES</u> - Establish goals and objectives for the product.
      A. Financial/ unit sales goals
      B. Market share goals, including share by segment if appropriate
      C. Pricing strategy and goals
      D. Other goals - - e.g., direct-to-patient messaging, targeted account usage, market (geographic/ customer segment) acceptance measures, etc.

IV. <u>STRATEGIES</u> – List overall plans to accomplish goals.
      A. Product positioning statement
      B. Target audience(s)
      C. Key messages – overall and by customer group
      D. Promotional strategy – overall and by customer group
      E. Communication strategy
      F. Sales strategy
      G. Support needed to accomplish:
         1. Marketing research needs
         2. Clinical research needs
         3. R and D support
         4. Manufacturing support
         5. Sales training support

V. <u>TACTICS</u> - Specific activities done to support the strategy and accomplish the goals.
      A. Promotional theme (by customer target)
      B. Sales force tactics
      C. Marketing tactics
         1. Samples
         2. Journal advertising
         3. Direct mail
         4. Web strategies
         5. Educational programs
         6. Speakers bureau
         7. Clinical trial programs

VI. <u>BUDGETS</u>
    A. Sales force allocation and costs
    B. Marketing costs
        1. Promotion
        2. Advertising
        3. Mail
        4. Samples
        5. Literature
        6. Educational meetings
        7. Patient programs
        8. Other

CHAPTER 6

Product Phase-Out -- the Toughest Job

While product phase-out is one of the least favorite parts of the product manager job, it is a critical aspect of the business in terms of managing resources and profit. Thus, not only is it important for a product manager to understand how to identify and handle product phase-outs, but it is important to manage it well and with confidence in order to demonstrate a grasp of business fundamentals. To develop management potential and move up career-wise, directing a product phase-out well can be a great path to gain both experience and attention.

Phase-out checklist

What fundamentals need to be satisfied in order to manage a product phase-out 'well'? The following is a check list of areas to assess and work through in managing a phase out. There are other areas that may need to be addressed specifically within a product/ project, but this provides a good starting point.

1) Lifecycle assessment – is the product really ready for retirement or is there another alternative?
2) Customer review – how many customers use the product *routinely* now versus in the past? Are there large, influential users out there?
3) Inventory analysis –
    - Part A: Implant inventory – total amount, core versus outlier SKU supply, hidden 'pockets' around the globe, return policy, and expiration dates (if applicable)?
    - Part B: Instrument inventory – on the books and off (some may have been fully amortized), likely condition, ownership and return ability.

4) Market/ pricing analysis – are there any opportunities to *grow* in a specific market if price was slashed? Alternatively, if price was raised, how much business would be lost? How much cash generated?
5) Product cannibalization/ substitution – estimating issues/ concerns with moving customers to alternative products or with preventing customer from moving too quickly. Are there competitor products that may pose a problem in customer conversions?
6) Distribution decisions and timing – pruning and adding distribution to meet inventory, profit, sales goals and customer issues.
7) Promotion possibilities – to increase sales, decrease inventory, or help transition to the substitute product.
8) Communication to the field – managing the tricky conversation about cutting off product flow to customers.

The last component that takes shape occurs while investigating and choosing how to handle the other eight facets of the phase-out plan: the financial piece. This encompasses two phases. The first is putting together projections for how sales and profits will be impacted and estimating inventory write-offs and expenses associated with phase-out activities. The second phase is dynamic and flexible, consisting of options, opportunities, recommendations, and possibilities. It includes such things as outlines for specific actions to increase sales, delay the decrease of sales, increase profits, or minimize loss. Opportunities and possibilities that require funding but have potential financial and/or strategic value are often proposed and considered by executive management during phase-outs. This is because the appetite for risk may be larger, especially if the investment/ profit ratio is reasonable. Metrics under various categories such as price increases, distribution changes, and product substitution plans should all be included for management review as well.

Note: Even if your company does not formally have a product phase-out review process, it is a good idea to still document information and decision-making criteria so that you are prepared if/ when customers/ sales force conflicts or questions arise and management does suddenly get involved. Secondly, for large, complex phase-outs, taking the project through a modified stage-gate is a good way to ensure that the various parts of the company are aware and have received communication, and any underlying issues are exposed. This can save considerable heartburn and backtracking down the road. Plus, it is a great demonstration of your leadership skills.

Assessing lifecycle, customers, and competition

LIFECYCLE ASSESSMENT

The five stages of product lifecycle management are taught as fundamental marketing facts and most product managers can name them without much thought. (Just as a reminder: they are development, introduction/ launch, growth, maturity, decline/phase-out.) The issue with this concept however is that it sounds like every product marches through the phases in some form or fashion and there is little that can be done about it.

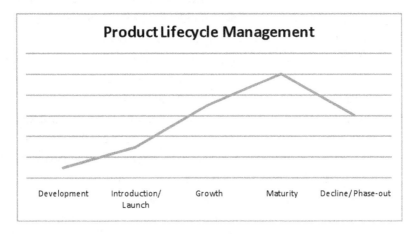

There is also a focus within medical devices particularly on 'innovation' or, as it is typically measured, on new product launches. This focus is based on the belief that new products are the lifeblood of medical devices and that product lifecycles are relatively short within the device industry as a whole – somewhere between three and five years on average. Thus, it is important for a company to continually develop and launch new products as the 'older' products fall into decline and effectively become 'obsolete.' Many companies measure percentage of sales that come from 'new products' versus total sales -- with the definition of 'new products' varying from company to company (but typically defined as either those launched within the last year or those launched within the last three years.)

As a product manager, responsible for the company's growth in sales and profit, how should you assess these beliefs and the resulting actions?

Well, as with so many accepted yet unsubstantiated 'facts,' some of these assumptions are generally true and reliable. However, this is not always and not necessarily true, which is where your expertise comes in.

New products do attract both sales force and customer attention, just as 'new' things tend to attract interest in virtually all settings. Thus, having a strong pipeline of products and concepts with innovations and features that meet (or better yet, exceed) the customer's needs and desires does provide opportunity to increase sales, and often can benefit profit as well.

Additionally, medical devices then will become obsolete and be replaced with newer technologies that are easier/ faster to use, better for the patient, or more cost-effective in some aspect. And, sometimes the amount of time for a technology to become obsolete is quite short. A company that is not willing to cannibalize and obsolete its own products will find that a competitor will do it quite willingly for them. Thus, there is a constant rise and fall of technology and a drive for improvement that can quickly make a device stale and stagnant within the marketplace, dooming it to the decline phase.

There is a catch, however. As discussed in an earlier chapter, products and even entire systems *can* be 'freshened' or 'updated' to keep pace with market trends and capabilities, as long as the core technology remains viable. The financial benefit to a 'refresh' versus a 'replace' can be tremendous, as long as sales continue to grow proportionately. This is because the cost in inventory, energy, and time of converting an existing customer to a new product has been foregone, and instead, the marketing, sales, and management teams can focus on converting new customers and retaining current ones.

For a product manager, it is important to call a spade a spade, and when it is time for a product to be phased out because it is taking up valuable time, money, and space with diminishing incremental return, then do the analysis and start putting together the phase-out plan. However, if there is a possibility of extending the product lifecycle – or if it is discovered that the disruption in customer relationships and sales is simply too costly at a particular point in time and needs to be postponed for other reasons, then look at options to add value to the product line via incremental technology additions/ updates, with the goal to change the product trajectory and extend the time in 'maturity' before ultimately moving into decline.

PRODUCT PHASE-OUT -- THE TOUGHEST JOB

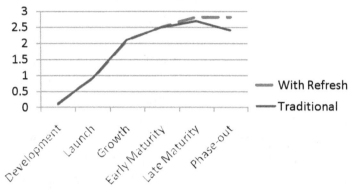

Lifecycle Chart: Impact of 'Product Refresh' on Sales

Customer assessment

Before making definitive plans, and definitely before engaging the sales team, the product manager needs to have a firm grasp on what happens with the product at a molecular level – who uses what, when, and how often. This data is not just a report to be run and looked at for the last three, six, or twelve months; it is also a foundational understanding of whose applecart you are about to upset. Thus, it is a good idea to know not only who is impacted and how much, but also *who they are* in the grand scheme of things. Is there a nationally-recognized surgeon, a friend of the CEO, a best buddy of the top sales representative for the last ten years running in the mix? If so, it is true that the decision should not necessarily change, but the approach almost certainly will need to be fine-tuned and handled carefully.

In addition, it is often useful to select a time when the product was in the early maturity phase and peaking to pull customer data and review usage. This provides a clear picture for comparison and can add facts and remove emotion from some conversations that may be difficult down the road. Product phase-outs take away a customer's favorite product and a sales representative's source of income. Both of these things produce strong reactions, so being prepared with data and with a clear picture of how flexible you and the company are willing to be in dealing with a tough situation is key.

During the customer assessment, it is a good idea to get a sense of how often a particular customer uses the product and in what situations. This is particularly important because it might be the critical piece of information down the road in determining how to best move forward.

As an example to illustrate importance, there was a shoulder implant system with very low usage except by a handful of surgeons across the U.S. Strategically, the company wanted to retain the option of moving forward in the shoulder implant market, but there was general consensus that this particular system was a 'dead horse.' However, two major shoulder surgeons with internationally known names and operating in a world-renowned center were in fact using the system fairly consistently, and the sales representative reported that they used it for more than eighty-five percent of their cases and were in the midst of a clinical study gathering long-term clinical data supporting its use. If the company discontinued the product, angering the two world-recognized surgeons and essentially dismissing their ongoing clinical study, then the company's ability to work with the surgeons was significantly compromised, plus the company's credibility in the shoulder marketplace could also be damaged. What should be done?

The product management team spent some time with both surgeons simply asking questions about their current product use, other systems/ products used, and indications/ rationale. Additionally, discussion about a more 'ideal' shoulder implant was initiated in order to draw out clinical experience, both in terms of outcomes data and O.R. particulars. The observations and conversations revealed that the surgeons used this system about fifty percent of the time, still significant usage but not quite what had been thought. Additionally, while their clinical data was strong, they did see the need for upgrades or other technology changes that were not forthcoming within the system, and thus were becoming increasingly dissatisfied.

This information enabled senior leaders at the company to approach the two surgeons about a change in strategic direction relating to shoulder implants, and that the current system would be phased out over a period of time. It was agreed that these two surgeons would continue to be primary customers of the system and be supplied for at least two more years while strategies were being set and decisions made. In return, the relationships between these influential surgeons and the company remained intact, but phase-out decisions were made as well.

Key take-away's:
1. Knowledge is key. First hand information is a must.

2. Relationships are invaluable, but note that it is a two-way street — there was real listening and a willingness to compromise, not just shove the company's decision through.
3. Senior management interaction may be required — even though the product manager did all the leg work, the physicians' wanted and needed to hear the commitment from senior management in order to finalize the deal.

COMPETITIVE ASSESSMENT: PRODUCT CANNIBALIZATION/ SUBSTITUTION

Whenever customers change products, there is a period of unrest when they consider alternatives. During this timeframe, there is a greatly increased risk of losing even a loyal customer. While you may have a product substitute that makes sense on the surface, each customer will evaluate other possibilities based on their own criteria, which will likely include factors other than product features and benefits alone.

The difficulty in estimating or predicting the product cannibalization/ substitution rate is that even the local sales representative (and sometimes especially the local sales representative) cannot provide a clear picture. Why is this? Because the representative is one of the factors that the customer may well consider, particularly if the customer has been looking for an 'excuse' to work more closely with another representative or to 'test out' whether another representative has the skills/ experience/ ability to handle some or all of the customer's business. The busier the customer, the more likely that he/ she will have relationships with multiple representatives and that at least one of them is waiting in the wings for an opportunity to emerge.

In the meantime, there is still the need to (more or less) accurately predict what the impact of phase out will be and where these customers are likely to go. Additionally, upticks in substitute product lines must be forecasted and planned for. So, what method should be applied to this apparent madness?

In many ways, this is simply a forecasting exercise. However, if the phase-out is large and covers multiple regions/ countries, be careful not to over-simplify it and fall into the trap of making large scale assumptions. The larger the product line, the bigger the scope, and the longer it has been on the market, the more discrete and individualized various areas/ territories will have become in how they perceive and handle the device and generalized 'rules' may or may not hold true.

So, let us walk through the steps to coming up with a phase-out substitution estimate based on a more complex, long-running product. However, this is an example only and will necessarily have to be tweaked in any real-world situation:

Step One: Break down customers/ markets into reasonable, manageable pieces.

This is NOT an attempt to manage each customer or find out exactly what they are likely to do, but simply to break the customer pool into a handful of discrete segments that can be looked at individually.

Example 1: Break down customers into the U.S., South and Central America, Europe, Asia, Australia, and rest of world. Thus, there are a total of six customer groups. Rationale for breaking customers down this way – each region/ area's customers represent a very different product mix, price point, and decision-making process. Thus, the factors for changing products and the phase-out process will necessarily be different. (Note that Canada and some other countries are not represented in the groupings. They can either be tossed in with a comparable market or have a separate category created if the customer pool is large enough.)

Example 2: Break down customers by product usage regardless of geography based on choices within the product line (i.e., cemented/ cement-less hip stems, cruciate-retaining/ posterior-stabilized knees, MIS/ open spine rod procedures). Rationale for this is that the substitution product may be quite different and even the reasons for customer use may vary widely, thus significantly impacting the factors in phasing-out.

Step Two: Brainstorm factors for each customer group that impacts the successful transition to the phase-out. Estimate the ideal substitute product choice and back-up choice from within your own product lines, then make a list of two to four competitive products that may also be 'in play.' (Remember to include regional choices that may not show up globally.)

The goal with this exercise is to have a draft list of issues/ factors that can both positively and negatively impact the customer (and perhaps the sales representative) in phasing out the existing product and transitioning the customer to the new product. The factors may end up virtually identical for all customer groups, but it will be highly unlikely that they will exert the same amount of 'pull' on each customer group.

Secondly, you need to know exactly where you expect this customer to end up from a product point of view, and whether there is another possibility within your own product line. You may find out there are multiple potential substitutes within your own products even. There also has to be recognition of the competitor's strength. This is especially important because you may come to realize that the competitor's product is stronger than your own 'substitute' (at least on the surface), which then must be addressed pro-actively.

> Example: Factors that can impact phase-out with a customer are long-term clinical results, comfort level with instruments, respect for design team/ product designer, full range of sizes, 'special' instruments/ implants made just for him/her, revision options, other customers/ surgeons in hospital/ area who also use product, OR team/ staff training and comfort level, cost and/or inventory issues and lots more. Brainstorming the top five to ten per region and prioritizing/ weighting provides a master list for assessment. Grade the to-be phased-out product against these criteria first to determine top score, then grade your and competitor's potential substitutes to spot strengths and issues.

Step Three: Assign probabilities to factor and/or stack rank them by customer group in order of importance. Include an estimate of customers who transition to substitute products versus competitor products.

Goal is to be able to assess what is most important to address and prioritize the top items for each customer group, with the hope that there is some overlap between groups and only five to eight items have to be dealt with. You may want to reach out to a small sample of customers or representatives within each group in order to help with this exercise, either while prioritizing or as a 'check' after doing so. This is particularly true both when you do not know the subject as well *and* when you have to develop a rapport with the management team later (sales or geographic management) on the phase-out plans.

It is highly likely that some percentage of customers will be 'lost' during the phase-out process. Pretending this will not happen is not only naïve, but it also ends up looking bad when numbers are not achieved because not all customers come along for the ride (either moving all or some of their business to a competitor.) At the very least, a best-case, worst-case, most-likely-case scenario should be developed to demonstrate percentage of customer loss possibilities and the resulting sales impact. Actions to mitigate this loss should be highlighted, and any weakness in substitute product versus the competitor (whether real or perceived) should also be discussed along with recommendations on how to handle.

Step Four: Settle on most-likely-case scenario by customer group with actions/recommendations agreed upon as the go-forward game plan for presentation to the appropriate internal teams for execution.

This is the final step before the execution phase – reviewing information with those running the tactical operations in manufacturing, sales, development, testing, etc.-anyone affected by the plan. Any feedback, issues, or concerns can then be raised and either addressed or debated. Forecast is then put into the system and the timeline for the phase-out is set.

Financials - balancing sales, profit, and inventory

INVENTORY ANALYSIS

One of the most important pieces of information in planning and executing a product phase-out is the inventory piece of the equation. Not only is it necessary for the financial analysis, but there are also many puzzle pieces that often come to light while locating and assessing inventory.

One of the first steps is determining whether the entire inventory is in known locations and accounted for. While this may seem obvious, if a system has been on the market for several years and if there have been several changes in distributors, then there may be inventory on the books that is unaccounted for. Additionally, it may also be that inventory *not* on the books is discovered. Most often this inventory will be mostly outlier parts and thus not helpful; however, it is better to discover and account for it on the front-end than have it show up later in the process unexpectedly. Additionally, there will probably be some 'bell curve' inventory that can be salvaged and used to manage supply with select customers.

There is also the possibility that significant amounts of inventory may exist while demand has dwindled, and the analysis may then turn to the possibility of re-purposing inventory for other markets. Often this takes the form of supplying product at very low cost/ price to specific international markets or for a bid situation (usually an international government). In this case, the inventory review also has to take a more detailed assessment of instruments, not only the number of instrument sets and their amortized value, but also whether they are in good enough condition to be re-used (or re-worked). Should this be the case, it entails a number of other processes involving quality, regulatory, and manufacturing, and will require a coordinated effort across the company.

Inventory Worksheet

Implant SKU's

	# of Items (A)	Cost per Item (B)	Total Cost = (A)*(B)
Part 1			
Part 2			
Part 3			
etc.			
TOTAL			

Instrument Sets

	# of Sets on Shelf (A)	# of Sets in Field (B)	Total # of Sets = (A)+(B)	Amortized Value of Sets $$	# of Sets-Amortized Value =$0
Instr Set #1					
Instr Set #2					
Instr Set #3					
etc					
TOTAL					

    One other aspect of inventory assessment to consider is ownership. In the U.S., the typical business model is to provide distributors and accounts with inventory on consignment. However, this is not always the case. Some older distribution agreements and some companies have purchase agreements either outright or over time with distributors to offset cost of instruments in particular. Additionally, many international distribution arrangements are based on purchase of instrument sets and implants, although there is a high degree of variability around how the implant transaction is handled. Return of implants during a phase-out may be written into agreements or may be a point of negotiation; however, knowledge of who owns the inventory should be sorted out as part of the initial review and analysis.

MEDICAL DEVICE MARKETING

BALANCING SALES AND PROFIT

There is the possibility that there is so much inventory, or a great imbalance of inventory weighted toward outlier sizes, such that inventory consolidation or even making some small manufacturing runs of additional 'bell curve' sizes may make sense. By doing so, incremental sales and profit can be generated, but *just as importantly*, overall inventory may be reduced even further by selling off outlier sizes as well. This has to be thought through as part of an overall strategy that considers distribution outlet, pricing for profit, and ensuring that the overall inventory build versus sell-off is worthwhile. However, one of the first steps in determining potential is to take a look at availability versus need, and assess against cost to build additional parts versus writing off excess items. Worksheets to look at implants and instruments are below, although they will need to be customized based on the specific system/ project.

Projected Additional Build

Bell Curve SKU's - Implant						
	# of Parts (A)	Avg Turns/ Mo (use based on 6 or 12 mos.) (B)	Months Inv. on Hand = (A)/(B)	Cost per Part (D)	Add'l Build to for Min Months On Hand* (E)	Add'l Build for Max Months On Hand* (F)
Part 1						
Part 2						
Part 3						
etc						
TOTAL						

* Calculate min/ max # of months based on # of SKU's with on-hand inventory. If 80-90% of parts have XX months on hand, select it as MIN. Determine MAX value by looking at roughly 50% of SKU's with inventory on hand for ZZ months.

Projected Write-Off's

Bell Curve SKU's - Implant					
	# of Parts (A)	Cost at Min = (D)*(E)	Cost at Max = (D)*(F)	Excess Inventory at Min ($)**	Excess Inventory at Max ($)**
Part 1					
Part 2					
Part 3					
etc					
TOTAL					

** For items that have MORE THAN enough parts to satisfy the 'months on hand' requirement, multiply by cost/ part to determine write-off.

Instrument Set Re-work Valuation

Instrument Sets

	# of Sets	Est. Rework Cost/ Set	# Needed	Investment Cost Total	Remaining Amortization Write-off
Instr Set #1					
Instr Set #2					
Instr Set #3					
etc					
TOTAL					

Marketing/ pricing analysis

In looking at the opportunities to make the most of the product during phase-out, there may be a chance to increase sales by raising price or taking the product into a new market. Note that this is actually part of a phase-out plan, not a 'refresh' option. The freedom of doing a phase-out means that small pockets of possibilities can be explored to grab the most value within the product and for the company.

There are two ways to go with pricing during a phase out – either up or down. Keeping the same price is an option, but the idea during a phase out is to either maximize sales via volume or price. The fastest way to do this is to change the price. Be aware that a combination of lowering price in one area of the product and raising it in another may be a viable combination as well. Analyzing current customer and market trends and potential usage may reveal possibilities, such as lowering price on standard items while raising it on outliers. Another possibility is to look at the procedure and consider pricing based on usage.

Price sensitivity is a factor to consider during analysis and investigation, but it may be tempting to be too conservative and not adjust enough to maximize impact. It may be possible to plan the phase out on a regional basis and/or test pricing hypothesis in specific markets before making a full-scale decision. Often, the rules-of-thumb that typically guide pricing (i.e., price should fall in line with competition or within the market valuation scale) are not true during a phase-out because you are not concerned with losing some customers due to higher prices, for instance.

Distribution decisions and timing

During phase-out, one of the more obvious aspects is that fewer and fewer sales representatives are selling the product. The corollary to this is equally obvious on reflection, but only on reflection. *Typically* fewer distributors are carrying the product line as well.

One way to look at timing product phase-out and manage down inventory is to move customers to another product *distributor by distributor*. The benefit of this is that the inventory can be reduced at the selected phase-out distributor sites and then consolidated to keep the remaining distributors/ customers supplied for much longer. So, as part of customer analysis and planning the timing of the phase-out, distributor pruning and inventory consolidation go hand-in-hand and can extend sales while bleeding off excess inventory.

Additionally, there may be a counter-intuitive argument to increase distribution in some cases and in some places. This may happen when a product is still considered desirable and 'state-of-the-art' in some parts of the world. Thus, it may make sense to phase-out a product in one location and replace it with something else, and then move the newly-freed instrument sets and inventory to a different location and actually use them to either expand a market, or even launch the product. This is highly dependent on the inventory supply; either there must be a significant amount of inventory on-hand that can be used or there is low-cost, un-used manufacturing capacity that can be dedicated without any other consequences.

Promotion possibilities

There are a couple of issues to consider during phase-out where a promotion may be worth considering:

1) There is quite a bit of excess inventory in some product area that could be easily used if only the sales force/ customers paid a bit more attention to it.

    (NOTE: If there is a predicate to this – such as there has to be more inventory produced, or a certain instrument is missing from most sets, then you do not have a promotion situation without first taking care of the predicate. Also, – it is almost always throwing good money after bad to spend more money in order to just throw away less inventory.)

2) The customers and/or the sales team are chomping at the bit to get the new/ substitute product and are likely to simply hold off, slow down, or stop using the current product that is being phased out while they wait for the new-and-improved product they do not have access to yet.

    (NOTE: And by doing so, they leave you holding a much higher amount of excess inventory than you want to and/or have planned for.)

In either of these situations, a promotion may well be worth investigating, either with a lot of bells and whistles or quite quietly and stealthily. In both cases, if you have a commission-based sales team, adding extra incentive often produces a speedy and satisfying result, although you have to take care that the incentive aligns with the outcome wanted. Some ideas for each are below, simply more to stimulate thought than provide specific direction since there are so many variables related to sales channel compensation and philosophy on customer interaction.

Sales team promotion ideas:

- Straight increase in commission for a period of time on the phase-out product, which can be by distributor if needed. It can also be handled as a percentage over prior year, over prior month, or as a percentage of sales/ budget to help in monitoring/ controlling.

    Example: If used as a percentage over something, then the representative has to achieve some specific amount (say a decline of no more than five percent loss over prior year) to get a five percent or more commission. If the representative achieves no more than a ten percent loss over prior year, then they get a two or more percent commission. If they lose more than ten percent over prior year, then they simply get their normal commission rate.

- Customer retention/ transition bonus – if the representative keeps the customer on the existing product for three months, then they get a retroactive bump in commission. If they successfully move the customer to the new/ substitute product, then they get an additional dollar amount as well.

    Example: Customer continues to use product over the three month timeframe specified as shown by sales per month steadiness. During the three months, the representative is paid regular commission, but at end of three months, the representative is paid retro-active five percent commission on either all or part of three months sales. For the transition part, if the surgeon's business at either three or six months is the same (or more?) than the prior three or six months' sales, then the representative is paid a transition bonus of $2500.

Communication externally – to the field and to the customers

The five 'W's' of journalism apply here, along with the other, universal W.

Bottom line, communication is absolutely critical for a phase out, but it is also tricky. Bring the sales team into the loop too soon, and you will find that you are fighting an uphill battle before you have even figured out what hill you are trying to climb. Bring them in too late, and your opportunity to both fine-tune the plan and engage them in a positive conversation is lost.

Steps to communication are as follows – virtually always, although there are exceptions. Keep in mind that if you end up talking to a distributor or sales representative, you need to go ahead and bring the sales management team into the loop. If you have a heart-to-heart with a customer, unless it is your best-friend (as defined by someone who was in your wedding), then you have essentially communicated to the sales team and need to 'step up' to bring the sales force into the loop. Be careful...be very, very careful. There are no innocent conversations when it comes to phase-outs. You are talking about taking a product away that customers use happily and with which the sales team supports their family. It is serious business for them – and should be for you too.

Steps for communication:

1) Phase-out plan is outlined, internal team, including executive group, is in alignment. Some issues likely still remain, but the big problems (are we even going to do this? Dr. XYZ uses it and may have a fit, etc.) have already surfaced and it is *still* a 'go'.

2) Put together a short presentation overview about the phase-out rationale, timeline, substitute product(s), major issues and actions/recommendations together. Include proposal for communicating to sales representatives and to customers directly and how 'upset customers' will be addressed (i.e., the 'easy button' for sales representatives) if possible. Ideally this presentation is no more than five slides; most of the information is in your head, not printed on the slide.

3) Meet with sales executive, usually VP of sales to review phase-out if he/ she is not already in the loop and find out how he/ she wants information communicated to sales management team. Go through presentation draft.

4) Set up meeting(s)/ call(s) with sales management to go through presentation and answer questions. Make sure you know where you still need their input; solicit help in fine-tuning. Be prepared for some pushback, but also make sure to talk about sales team/ customers that may pose problems in their area and discuss specific ways to handle. (This may have a part A and part B if there is a sales management executive structure such as Regional VP's and

then a sales management local structure such as distributors/ sales managers.)

- Make sure you have done your homework or have relevant examples from their territory to discuss. Bring spreadsheets with the 'sales/ customer' data to refer to if needed.
- Break the communication/ meeting/ information into small pieces. Ideally talk to each region/ group separately and not the whole team all together (i.e., the U.S. together or Europe together is harder than broken into regions/ countries). This is because a 'gang' mentality can quickly form as issues and concerns are raised, and you want the interaction to remain on an even keel and be a true back-and-forth exchange.
- If you are forced into a large group presentation, however, then try to talk to one or two sales executives/ key players separately ahead of time, with the purpose of getting their feedback and their support. Also, incorporate separate territory/ regional discussions and reviews into the game plan and present this early on as part of the feedback loop, with timeframes and assignments. This cuts down on miscellaneous murmuring and encourages the group toward action instead.

5) Initiate communication with sales team based on whatever game plan is agreed upon. Ideally the sales management is also engaged. Again, make sure you know where you want their input in fine-tuning the plan, and also solicit expertise in when/ how to approach their customer. (Some time may pass between steps four and five, depending on the organization.)

6) Communicate with customers per plan. Here are some possible types of communication, which can be and often are combined. Remember the more likely the customer is to be upset, the more personal the communication should be.

- Corporate communication – can take the form of a letter, e-mail, or even phone call. Ideally from the president of the company, but it may be spread out to others in the executive team based on relationships or simply due to time constraints. The communication should include some type of explanation, an apology for inconvenience along with a touch of sympathy, and a clear message for what the customer should do (use the substitute product). There should also be a very straightforward

path should the customer want to complain or otherwise engage directly with the company, taking some of the burden off the sales representative and preserving the service relationship.
- One-on-one visit – usually a VP or some member of the executive team, although can be anyone from sales or product management. The message is similar to above, although perhaps more personal and more engaged. If possible, demonstrate the substitute product and assist the representative with the transition. If there is a strong relationship historically, or even based on a current project interaction, these ties should be utilized.
- Via the sales team – a visit or call from the local/ regional sales management is not necessarily the best pathway, but with a broad-scale phase-out or large geographic area to cover, it may be reality. Make sure the person visiting the physician has an outline/ script of points to cover and a clear understanding of when and how to escalate should the physician have an issue.

NOTE – steps five and six may happen over time, particularly if the phase-out takes place distributor by distributor.

Here are the Five 'W's' for which to prep when talking to the sales team; this is more directed toward a local distributor or sales representative. There are the 'big picture' elements and then the 'small picture' local parts. Communication should touch both scales; the representative may only have immediate interest in his/ her part of the 'small' picture, but needs to know the 'big' picture in order to understand the overall rationale and to grasp the longer term implications. Both parts are integral to gaining enrollment in the vision and getting the representatives to get onboard with the program.

	Big Picture	Smaller Picture
Why?	Why is this worth doing at all?	Why are you doing this to me?
Who?	Who exactly approved this (and to whom could I complain and get it overturned if needed)?	Who is impacted in my turf?

PRODUCT PHASE-OUT -- THE TOUGHEST JOB

What?	What exactly is the game plan?	What are you planning to do about me/my customer/ my income and future? (i.e., what are the substitute products and how are you going to help with transition?)
When?	I do not really care unless I'm first in the phase-out or last to get the new product. Then the *when* is a big deal.	When is this going to happen and when do I get specific details? (which really means how long do I have to make sure my complaints are heard, if needed)?
Where?	Is this just me or other places as well?	Exactly where? (Which really means – am I being singled out?)

Final 'W' is (as always) – WIFM?? This is the one that you have to be able to answer at every level within the sales team, especially because they are giving something up. Not only do the sales representative and distributor give up income during the phase-out process, but he/she also gives up control, plus the risk of losing creditability with a customer is tremendous and quite scary. Being knowledgeable of that undercurrent and respectful as well is not only the right thing to do, but also the best way to negotiate some rocky, and sometimes shaky, ground.

Successfully staging and managing a product phase-out from proposal through approval and communication, down to the execution details, demonstrates strength and ability to deliver on a vision. It is because of the breadth and depth of skill required that product phase-outs are so challenging and great career-builders as well.

CHAPTER 7

What Does it Take to be a Product Manager in Medical Device?

The competition to land a position in medical device product management is tough. Not only is it fulfilling to help others (patients and providers), but it is also a good career from the perspective of compensation and opportunity for travel and personal growth. If it is your goal to have a career in the field of medical device marketing, then you need to develop skills and experience that you can use to translate into demonstrated ability to do the job.

The product manager role

PREPARATION AND PERSPIRATION

Awareness of the specific skills required and then finding assignments that demonstrate financial acuity, presentation skills, sales ability, etc. is the best avenue to gaining experience, without actually having the job. Pick five to seven of these job performance aspects that you want to showcase, and document both your role and your results so that you can talk about them within context of things you have accomplished. Additionally, know that breaking into medical device marketing is highly competitive, and it may take several tries before you land the position. You may have to make a lateral move, and many people have even taken a step down in order to get the role. Your genuine desire to get into the industry and the marketing field has to come across; a lot depends on what you want.

As with most jobs, there is the job description, and then there is the job. To make sure 'product manager' is really the role for you, here is an insider look at the role, in addition to the official description. Use this information to confirm that this is really the position for you:

- First, a product manager is a bit of an adrenaline-junkie...during the day, things will not ever be predictable, follow priorities, or go the way they are supposed to go. If you cannot juggle and love it, this is not the job for you, but if you get bored easily and can analyze to shift priorities (and you realize that emergency does not always equal priority), then it is a great career.
- Second, it is important to build relationships with everyone and not ever burn a bridge. This is an incestuous industry and once you have been in it for over five years, you will find that you know many people who can either help or hurt your career; you want them to know who you are and want to help you. No one ever really goes away, they just relocate. Even if you never come across that person again, they will still know someone who knows someone.
- Third, a product manager can talk to customers with the sales guys and talk shop with manufacturing. This is not only an integral part of the job, but also essential in building relationships because these are the two areas that can save you (or the product, sales, etc.) when all else goes wrong. The time will come when you need each; if they know and respect you (and vice versa), it makes a world of difference.
- Last, a product manager has an ability to absorb and translate technical information in such a way that it is both intuitive and compelling to the audience. In addition to going into surgery, the product manager is the interpreter between the engineering team and the sales force. You must be able to really grasp the testing, surgery, and design rationale information, as well as lead in the development of the core message about the product/ system. Then you have to break it down into comprehensive, manageable segments for the sales team to absorb. The higher your ability to talk at a technical level, yet still connect with your audience, the greater your value will be.

DAY-TO-DAY: WHAT DOES A PRODUCT MANAGER REALLY DO?

In summary, the product manager's role is top line and bottom line. Like the sales team, marketing is to focus on sales (top line). Like operations, the focus should always also be on profit (bottom line). Balancing the two is a bit like walking on a high wire, and figuring out how to do so in different situations is always a challenge. Of course, that is what makes the position always an adventure.

WHAT DOES IT TAKE TO BE A PRODUCT MANAGER IN MEDICAL DEVICE?

At the end of the chapter, there are several formal job descriptions. For a better look at the day-to-day life of the product manager's job, however, the following section perhaps gives a more down-to-earth view of the activities and the balancing act required.

The product manager's job is to…

Drive Sales:

1. Understands the sales process

    Knows <u>who</u> the customer is, <u>how</u> the purchase is completed, <u>why</u> purchase from XYZ company, and <u>what</u> criteria are used for the purchase decision
    - Provide sales support (literature, samples, digital media, etc.)
    - Assist sales representatives in moving surgeons along the funnel to evaluations and then to close.

    How?
    - Time with sales representatives and sales management
    - Phone calls/listening to complaints
    - Testing literature/media
    - Time in surgery/understanding demands on a successful representative

2. Identifies <u>needs</u>/predicts values

    Analysis of market, with emphasis on finding pockets of opportunity and then placing bets/ gambling on where the company can grow
    - Determines what is needed to grow sales faster. This can be a <u>product</u> or something else (like a marketing campaign or a promotion).
    - Provides analysis along with business plan to gain company-wide support. Uses both primary and secondary data points.

    How?
    - Listens to customers (surgeons and sales representatives)
    - <u>Watches</u> customers (observation is the key to finding opportunity)
    - Open to change/opportunity
    - Digs for numbers and/or facts
    - Cross-references data points (no favorite source)
    - Takes a stand, makes a bet, but with analysis

3. Serves in a liaison role to keep balance and provide perspective

    Acts as the conduit between inside the company and outside, balancing technical and business aspects while maintaining clear focus on patient outcomes and ethical standards.

- Business check to design team
- Technical interface to sales team
- Corporate connector to key surgeons

How?
- Part of the design team, but role is to ensure that <u>market</u> needs are met, product being designed is marketable and makes financial sense (i.e., consider inventory, etc.)
- Product/area technical expert to provide sales support and training. Can describe technical information in plain English; make it a "story."
- Provides input on design teams, visits surgeons (and in some company's manages contracts)

And Make a Profit:

1. Manages inventory via accurate forecasting, guidelines for set turns/ field use, and appropriate loaners/ demonstration kits.

    Everyday decisions on existing products determine short and longer term manufacturing plans, which in turn impacts resourcing and profitability
    - Responsible for money tied up in field inventory and in pipeline build.
    - Considers obsolete inventory. $$ that are essentially 'trash' because it will be years before it is used.

    How?
    - Understands how sets are used and determines appropriate turn ratios. Supports field with loaner program.
    - Forecasts based on stream of current market information, not budget
    - Works with planners to periodically asses and "bell curve" usage and adjust

2. Carefully plans and implements launches to minimize inventory impact and maximize price.

    Understands that forecasting and inventory planning with the sales team during product launch can make a tremendous difference in product profitability.
    - Most impact on product line profit is during launch, Inventory built during launch is typically the highest percentage of obsolete product.
    - Gets competitive data on pricing – list and ASP – from all sources

available. Determines price tier desired and regional variation possibilities. Develops pricing discount/ commission ratio matrix.

How?
- Enrolls sales management/ sales team early into plan to gain information and maximize price, reduce inventory
- Uses limited (early) release to learn sizing bell curve/outlier sizes
- Gains input from sales team and OR staff on how instruments are used and how cases can be laid out.
- Reviews implant needs to minimize launch inventory and pipeline build.

3. Maximizes budget impact without going over amount.

Budgets are nearly always less than ideal, yet you are accountable for results; creatively finding a way to deliver within the framework provided is part of the real world
- Plans for the year in advance and then is flexible based on new ideas
- Has a stated purpose for money spent and measure of the success

How?
- Plans to find synergies with other product areas and combines funds
- Clever and different campaigns attract attention; considers the audience and how to stand out from the crowd
- Invites people from all areas to contribute when trying to make a BIG impact. The best ideas often come from unexpected places.

THINKING ABOUT THE ROLE A BIT DIFFERENTLY

The product manager role is compared to many things, all of which contain a grain of truth and none of which are exactly right. In some companies some of the descriptions are more 'correct' than others, while other companies tend to view the role a different way. However, regardless of the company, a situation will arise that requires the product manager to step outside his/her typical comfort zone of action and thought and think/ act differently. At those times in particular, it is good to have some different paradigms to draw from.

1) Product manager as the CEO and visionary – oversees top line and bottom line (sales/ P and L) and scans horizon for future

In this comparison, the position has the responsibility of ensuring ultimate success of the product(s)/ system(s), regardless of what exactly is needed to make that happen. However, a critical difference is that *responsibility* and *accountability* do not equal *authority*, at least in the sense of 'command and control.'

While the product manager is expected to deliver results, they do not have direct line reports across the company. Instead, the key skills are influence, force of will and personality, sheer determination, plus an ability to know when to tread with tact and when to escalate an issue.

Bottom line: mentally accept that accountability and leadership go hand-in-hand, and can accomplish far more than lines on an organization chart.

2) Product manager as the hub of the wheel – connector of internal/ external functions

The idea is that the product manager is at the center of the wheel and all the other departments are the spokes leading out to the rim.

The product manager/ marketing interacts with all other aspects of the company, connecting them in an integral and balanced way to ensure that the 'wheel' stays rounded and that the project/ product/ company can continue to move forward. This vital function keeps all external areas (sales, customers, market research) moving in sync with internal areas (finance, supply chain, manufacturing, R and D).

This model highlights one of the drawbacks to the product manager position – namely that each functional area only intersects with the product manager on a limited basis, either directly if the product manager is needed or indirectly if marketing assists in answering a question or connecting areas (such as in tracking down inventory, handling quality issues, involvement in a development project). This in essence means that each area interacts with the product manager/ marketing only for a small slice of the overall 'pie,' and thus typically underestimates the amount and type of work marketing does.

Bottom line – marketing is not the place to be if you need constant recognition and reassurance of your worth because most of the folks with whom you work will only be aware of some of what you do…and will not even fully value everything they know because it is not meaningful to them.

3) Product manager as a bridge and bridge-builder – provides flow of information into and out of organization

The product manager is builder and maintainer of links that provide the critical flow of information and communication needed to sustain and grow the organization. This is akin to the circulatory system in that the ability to gather information, make reasonable deductions, and effectively communicate intentions and messages are absolute requirements for an organization to decide strategy and implement tactics.

Understanding where the 'bridges' or links are needed, how to develop them, and then using them effectively is seen as the product manager's core role in bringing together disparate pieces inside the company.

Bottom line: this is a great visual representation, but difficult to achieve as an individual and works best when networks can be linked together to leverage both relationships and information.

4) Product manager as captain of the ship – sets direction and steers the course

In this iteration, the product manager sets the course and determines where the 'ship' will go, working with the team (ideally) to set the roadmap and chart progress. The 'ship' itself is determined by the company; in some cases it is the project/ product, while in others it can be as large as setting the strategic direction.

One thing to be aware of in this version of the role is that the 'captain' cannot sail the ship alone, and while on the high seas the captain may be the law, judge, and jury, there typically has to be much more reasonableness and interaction with the 'crew' in the real world in order to be effective.

Bottom line – being the leader takes more than simply snapping out orders, no matter how appealing that may sound; rather, enrolling the team into the vision of the journey and soliciting their thoughts will likely lead to a more sound plan and a faster 'voyage.'

Sales and marketing – working together

CLASSICAL MARKETING VERSUS THE REAL WORLD

Classical marketing teaches that sales is a function of marketing and thus sales activities are supposed to be directed by the marketing team. Real life in medical devices teaches a bit different story. It is the exception for sales in medical devices to actually function as an arm of marketing. Rather, the sales team is seen and most often acts as an independent area, as separate in action and day-to-day task as manufacturing or development.

At the same time, this does not mean that marketing and sales are truly entirely separate functions and really are un-related. Rather, it is critically important to recognize that sales are an extremely important metric of success, and often the most important measure within a company. Not only is it relatively easy to track success/ failure, but also ultimately sales are in fact the lifeblood of the company. Having respect for the sales team, even while understanding that many in sales will not fully understand and appreciate the value or need for marketing, makes a world of difference in building a bridge and enabling a positive working relationship.

TENSION BETWEEN SALES AND MARKETING – A GOOD THING?

So – what about tension between sales and marketing? It exists at most companies, although in some cases the volume can be dialed up so high that communication is virtually non-existent and even minor issues become explosive. Is it a problem, and if so, how do you handle it?

First, it is important to recognize that a level of tension between sales and marketing exists *naturally*. This is because the sales department focuses on the top line, with the goal of driving dollars regardless of the cost. While marketing also cares deeply about the top line, there is responsibility for the bottom line profit as well that drives a focus on balancing incremental sales against the cost of obtaining those dollars. This is why marketing is key in setting price and discount policy, as well as overseeing bundling and promotions, and determining where resources are directed for future growth.

However, while the natural tension between unconstrained sales growth and ensuring profitability should be evident, it should not be disrespectful or cause constant storms. Instead, the level of tension *should* be the source of continued conversations and require sales and marketing to work together in order to maximize sales and profitability, with both sides communicating openly about opportunities and goals.

Overall, a balance of tension is ideal, enough that sales growth is encouraged but profit is also highly valued. If too much tension is the norm, then communication grinds to a halt with minor concerns blowing up into major controversies and 'secret' deals are cut as turf wars escalate to see who really runs the show. If no tension is evident, it is generally indicative that sales is running the show and profit takes a backseat to sales growth. When this happens, there are usually other indicators as well – such as sales determines the product portfolio plan/ priorities and strategy becomes indistinguishable from tactics. In this case, marketing has lost its way and is not functioning as an integral leader in the organization.

Critical skill sets

In putting together a resume of experience that demonstrates capability to function in the product manager role, there are three major abilities that every company looks for. The specific expertise needed and areas where it should be applied differ to some degree in each company, although there is definitely significant overlap in knowledge areas.

Technical

This is a controversial topic because many marketers believe that their expertise is in business decision-making and developing messaging/ branding and support material for their product/ system. However, it is the marketing person who stands between the engineer and the sales team, reducing volume and translating content to make it accessible. It is at best extremely difficult and at worst virtually impossible for the product manager to do his/her job well without a good understanding of the technical details of their product line, indications, anatomy, etc.

Additionally, for a product manager to be respected by either the engineering team or the sales force, speaking intelligently in 'his/her world' is an absolute must. This takes two forms – each requiring enough understanding of the technical terminology and concepts that the product manager can readily absorb and synthesize alternatives and differing perspectives in order to participate, and sometimes mediate, the conversation. The first forum requirement is to handle direct, dynamic conversation with engineers and/ or with the sales team. The second situation is similar but with the addition of a customer to the discussion, with the expectation that the product manager not only fully join in the discussion but also *add real value* to the conversation.

In the first scenario, the product manager has to enter fully into development conversations, answer technically-based questions, and be able to both form and defend opinions regarding the product/ procedure, the message, and future needs/ direction. Passing the 'test' in the first scenario is required before an engineer wants a product manager around with a customer and before a sales representative even allows the product manager to have contact with his/ her customer (and source of income). Without learning the technical side of the business, the product manager cannot earn the trust of either group and merely skims the surface, parroting phrases and thoughts borrowed from others. Leading the team (either engineering team or sales team) in strategic evaluations or in tactical execution will not be possible unless they believe that you know what you are talking about and also believe that you will appreciate what they have to say as well.

FINANCIAL

The product manager is the eyes and ears of the executive team, and sometimes the mouth as well. However, it is up to the product manager to effectively communicate both the current state of affairs and future recommendations clearly. What is the best way to do this? Numbers are the clearest and most effective form of communication in many cases, especially with the executive group. Looking at sales, profit, inventory, distribution, etc. with both financial history and projections that support the plan ensure that the product manager is both heard and understood.

There is also an absolute requirement that a product manager must be able to put together and defend a well-researched business plan that assesses the market, the competition, and the company resources. In order to do the research and develop the plan, there has to be a well-developed ability to analyze and assess numerical data. The product manager has to synthesize all the external information, combine it with internal company resources and competencies, and then ideally add in information and instinct to create a complete picture of the specific opportunity and recommendation.

In fact, four chapters in this book have sections related to financial analysis, targeting, pricing, and forecasting. Competency in the financial arena is a critical skill set to develop and continue to hone even once in a product manager role. The more comfortable you are in pulling together data from multiple sources and assessing it as an ongoing exercise, the better you will be able to make your case, as well grasp and present relevant information.

COMMUNICATION

Virtually every product manager job description talks about communication and wants proof of both written and oral competency. Being able to talk to people in a way that they understand and relate to you is important in many jobs, but it is probably <u>the</u> most critical skill in the product manager role, surpassing all the others combined. This is because beyond all else, the product manager is a connector – as seen in all four analogies, whether the CEO, wheel hub, bridge, or ship captain – and for the connection to be effective, it must pull people together and get them to understand each other as well.

The product manager stands in the gap to bring people and information together in ways that they need to hear and/or see it so that it is easily understood and acted upon. This can happen both informally in conversation or in meetings, or formally in presentations to small groups or to larger audiences. The best product managers bring not only clarity, but also a passion and enthusiasm that cause others to climb onboard and join in as well.

Thus, it is more than just conveying information; it is also connecting links and imparting a sense of urgency that causes a group to organize or shifts an organization into gear. Think about what needs to happen – the approval or buy-in needed, the energy surge desired, the team unity, etc. – when communicating and plan accordingly. Most of all, remember the most important feature of all: the WIFM factor. Think like the people you are addressing and make sure it is going to make sense to them, not that it just sounds good to you.

Last words...

A few final thoughts on how to be the best product manager and leader possible...
- Do not get stuck on HOW things are done, focus on WHAT needs to happen and WHEN. The HOW is a sticky trap that detracts from results and opens the door to excuses.
- Ask targeted questions that challenge assumptions and the status-quo. Avoid falling into the 'must-be' trap by defining high risk or life-and-death scenarios that cause others to step outside the rules. When people start

saying 'well if we ignore this, then we could', you are on the right track – it is easy to pull back and eliminate options after the brainstorming door has been opened.
- Do not be afraid of asking others. Use the expertise inside and outside the company. There is no harm in listening, even if you think you already know the answer, plus someone else may offer an idea that refines or alters for the better.
- Shield your team from the outrageous and ridiculous, both criticisms and demands. Keep them focused on the WHAT and WHEN, not on the extraneous.
- All talk and no action makes for a poor leader and a poor example. Jump in and lend a helping hand. Not only will it energize the team, it also ensures you *really* understand and keeps your knowledge relevant.

Appendix

Below are four sample job descriptions for product manager roles at various levels. The purpose is to give you an idea of the core essentials of the product manager role, regardless of level, and the skills/ expectations that are added or increase as you go up the ladder.

Please note that these are only examples and wide variations will exist across companies, both the requirements for levels and the responsibilities. This is only intended for reference and to help guide if you are developing a plan for going into medical device marketing.

Associate Product Manager
The Associate Product Manager (APM) is responsible for providing product management and marketing support to specific product lines in accordance with the strategy developed by the Product Management Team. The APM will be expected to work closely with other key functional areas, including Clinical, Regulatory, Development, Operations, and Sales to accomplish the goals and objectives established for the product.

Requirements	Responsibilities
<ul><li>Bachelor degree in business or related field is required; MBA is preferred.</li><li>Demonstrated strong work ethic and initiative in accomplishing objectives of the position</li><li>Effectively build and maintain positive relationships with peers and colleagues across organizational levels.</li><li>Superior written and verbal communication skills.</li><li>Key performance areas include product management, ability to launch products, ability to track and report on status of product activity.</li><li>Working knowledge of Windows, Microsoft Office (Word, PowerPoint, Excel, and Outlook).</li><li>Excellent verbal presentation and written communication skills.</li><li>Excellent organizational skills and decision-making ability.</li><li>Detail oriented and team player.</li><li>Ability and initiative to work productively in the following environments:<ul><li>» ambiguous</li></ul></li></ul>	<ul><li>The APM has primary responsibility for management of activity that is directly related to the product itself. This includes:<ul><li>» Sales and customer support</li><li>» Surgical case observation and coverage when necessary</li><li>» Participation in cadaver based training and product development labs</li><li>» Product training</li><li>» Development of product related collateral materials (surgical techniques, brochures, models, product bulletins, videos, etc.)</li><li>» Product communication, to sales force and customers. This includes newsletters, electronic media, voicemail, group mailings, etc.</li><li>» Management of individual product-focused projects (prioritization of engineering work, product definitions, etc.)</li><li>» Inventory management and control in conjunction with operations</li><li>» Tracking and evaluation of product performance</li></ul></li></ul>

» fast paced » hands-on » deadline dictated • Requires at least 30% travel that will include weekends.	» Representation of product at trade shows » Communicate product updates » Develop and maintain relationships with surgeons and sales reps » Other duties as assigned by the Senior PM. • The APM is responsible for timely and appropriate reporting of progress (and sensitive situations) on above items to the manager. • Primary responsibility for work at the financial planning and strategic and business management level is assigned at Product Manager level or higher. These responsibilities may be delegated to APM as deemed appropriate by the manager.

Product Manager
The Product Manager (PM) is responsible for providing product management and marketing support to specific product line(s) in accordance with the strategy developed by the Marketing Management Team. It is PM's responsibility to use all available data sources (market research, financial analyses, market trends, competitive intelligence, etc.) to achieve product line(s) sales and profit objectives. The PM will be expected to work closely with other key functional areas, including Clinical, Regulatory, Development, Operations, and Sales to accomplish the goals and objectives established for the product.

Requirements	Responsibilities
• Bachelor degree in business or related field is required; MBA is preferred.	• Manage a product line to achieve sales and operating profit objectives.

- Minimum of three-four (3-4) years experience in marketing, product management involving product development, proven accomplishments in project management in the medical or surgical products industry; or equivalent combination of education and experience.
- Expertise with Microsoft Outlook, Excel, Word and PowerPoint
- Knowledge of medical device industry and products
- Ability to travel over 35% of the time that will include weekends.
- Demonstrated strong work ethic and initiative in accomplishing objectives of the position
- Effectively build and maintain positive relationships with peers and colleagues across organizational levels.
- Able to present effectively to management.
- Superior written and verbal communication skills.
- Able to manage budget. Can analyze business, develop solutions and implement them within budgetary constraints.
- Capacity for strategic thinking, planning, project management and product development.
- Analyze the positioning of products and competitors to identify strategies for differentiation and increased sales and share.
- Review current business for potential line extensions or new use development programs.
- Manage the initiation and development of new and existing product lines.
- Know and follow all laws and policies that apply to one's job, and maintain the highest levels of professionalism, ethics and compliance at all times.
- Performs other special projects and functions as assigned by the department manager.
- Champion the product lifecycle process, including new product identification, product development, product launch and market management.
- Identify new product ideas that address unmet clinical needs or represent material improvements to standard of care through insightful investigations with clinician customers, field sales representatives, engineers and scientists.

- Responsible for developing and supporting training and education of internal employees; core marketing and sales collateral materials; timely responses for requests for product positioning; and annual planning and forecasting of sales.
- Demonstrated consistent ability to deliver results across multiple projects.
- Knowledge and experience with new product development and introduction processes are essential.
- Must have a sound technical understanding of surgery and the O.R. environment.
- A background in hospital-based sales models is highly preferred.
- Experience interacting directly surgeon customers greatly desired.
- Ability to work collaboratively and independently in a cross-functional and team oriented environment is essential.
- Ability to deliver results with multiple and complex projects.

- Prioritize and select products for advancement through development process through business case assessment, using cross functional resources to understand regulatory, reimbursement, professional education, legal, and operational implications of product strategies.
- Develop product portfolio strategies that maximize sales force effectiveness and overall penetration of innovative technologies.
- Lead cross functional team(s) in all activities that will deliver products on time to the market that improve patient outcomes and increase customer satisfaction.
- Build powerful relationships with key thought leaders in spine community.
- Manage clinical data efforts along with clinical champions for marketed products.
- Monitor competitive activity to identify potential threats, while uncovering and exploiting opportunities arising from industry trends.
- Other duties as assigned.

◀ MEDICAL DEVICE MARKETING

Senior Product Manager	
\multicolumn{2}{l}{The Senior Product Manager (SPM) will be responsible for establishing and driving product marketing strategies and programs consistent with overall business objectives for their assigned product area. This will be done by utilizing innovative approaches to traditional marketing tools and methodologies. This position serves as a mentor to other marketing professionals and requires minimal supervision.}	
\multicolumn{2}{l}{The SPM will be expected to work closely with other key functional areas, including Clinical, Regulatory, Development, Operations, and Sales to accomplish the goals and objectives established for the product.}	
Requirements	Responsibilities
<ul><li>Bachelor degree in business or related field is required; MBA is preferred.</li><li>Minimum of five-seven (5-7) years experience in marketing, product management involving product development, proven accomplishments in project management in the medical or surgical products industry; or equivalent combination of education and experience.</li><li>Expertise with Microsoft Outlook, Excel, Word and PowerPoint</li><li>Knowledge of device industry and products</li><li>Ability to travel over 35% of the time that will include weekends.</li><li>Demonstrated strong work ethic and initiative in accomplishing objectives of the position</li><li>Efficiently manage a large workflow and multiple projects at one time</li></ul>	<ul><li>Develops product and marketing strategies within a product segment or marketing function</li><li>Develops and executes product marketing strategies to achieve stated revenues and market share objectives.</li><li>Uses Business Intelligence skills to evaluate market trends and develop segment penetration opportunities and targets.</li><li>Works with outside agencies and organizations to benchmark marketing programs and brings best practices in-house.</li><li>Oversee process resulting in consistent positioning and branding image throughout product lines, promotional materials and marketing/sales events.</li><li>Ensures product and marketing messaging throughout all communication mediums in order to deliver clear product education and support.</li></ul>

- Effectively build and maintain positive relationships with peers and colleagues across organizational levels.
- Develops relationships with executive team; able to effectively bring ideas, proposals and business cases forward for consideration.
- Superior written and verbal communication skills.
- Demonstrated capability of developing and managing surgeon relationships.
- Analytical and budgetary experience; able to comprehend, analyze and develop solutions for complex problems that shape business strategy and implement them within budgetary constraints.
- Possess technical abilities to interact with both outside medical professionals and internal development teams.
- A confident and persuasive manager with leadership and team building abilities across all levels of the organization.
- Proven marketing management performance within the surgical segment with a strong clinical orientation.
- Capacity for strategic thinking, planning, project management and product development.
- Experience assisting sales team with the sales of new systems and upselling existing clients

- Collaborates with field sales management, consulting surgeons and patients to design, evaluate and validate marketing strategies and programs.
- Supports the sales force in achieving metrics, sales targets, new product launches, closing new customers.
- Responsibilities include Product Development Strategy, Brand Management, Strategic Planning, Pricing and Inventory Plans, Key Surgeon Relationships, and Sales Force Support.
- Will be aware of and play an active role in product acquisition efforts.
- Will ensure the timely response to assigned surgeon consultants and manage interactions with consultants in accordance with Code of Ethics/ AdvaMed.
- Responsibility for developing and supporting training and education of internal employees; core marketing and sales collateral materials; timely responses for requests for product positioning; and annual planning and forecasting of sales.
- Position may include management of a direct report

Marketing Director

High visibility leadership position requiring management and/or coordination of cross-functional product development, operational, and agency teams. Role also requires significant consensus- and influence-building among field sales personnel and key customers. Responsible for coordinating product development, as well as devising and managing marketing, education, support, forecasting/inventory and distribution programs to achieve the objectives of the respective business line. Overall management of product management function across multiple product lines and market segments within the respective Group. Responsibilities include coordinating strategic assessment, new product development, sales support, market/faculty development, and establishing the budget for activities related to the Group. Metrics for success include achieving sales, profit, and inventory targets as well as meeting product launch dates.

Requirements	Responsibilities
- Bachelor degree in business or related field is required; MBA is preferred. - Minimum of eight-ten (8-10) years experience in marketing, product management involving product development, proven accomplishments in project management in the medical or surgical products industry; or equivalent combination of education and experience. - Minimum of four-five (4-5) years in a supervisory/managerial role. Sales experience in medical/surgical products beneficial. - Superior written and verbal communication skills and the ability to develop them in others. - Ability to work effectively within existing management team and overall organization.	- Lead product management team in developing and executing marketing programs designed to increase adoption and utilization of products. - Provide strategic prioritization and market requirement inputs as part of business planning cycle. Responsible for coordinating marketing inputs on yearly sales budget. - Work closely with Development Engineering, Manufacturing, Regulatory, Sales, Finance and related departments to oversee project teams and meet project milestones. - Control the existing product lines specific to the Group, including recommendations for product line extensions and/or line trimming, forecasting, pricing strategies, literature/video/sales support materials, manufacturing support and customer service/operations support.

- Demonstrated capability of developing and managing surgeon relationships.
- Analytical and budgetary experience; able to comprehend, analyze and develop solutions for complex problems that shape business strategy and implement them within budgetary constraints.
- Successful history of leadership and management skills
- Excellent interpersonal skills across all levels of management
- Possess technical abilities to interact with both outside medical professionals and internal development teams.
- A mature confident and persuasive manager with strong leadership and team building abilities across all levels of the organization.
- Global Marketing experience required.
- Proven marketing management performance within the surgical segment with a strong clinical orientation.
- A demonstrated capacity for strategic thinking, planning, project management and product development.
- Solid understanding of overall market analysis, planning, development and management.
- Average travel requirement is approximately 35% that will include weekends.

- Ensure that the company maximizes and optimizes its performance and operating objectives in the specific segment through identification of market trends, competitive activities and business opportunities, and through the effective development and presentation of strategic, market and product development plans.
- Maintain key relationships to stay on the pulse of new market opportunities.
- Analyze new business opportunities and continually push for new innovations in existing market segments while developing long-term strategic plans for future development, acquisitions and or distribution agreements for new product offerings.
- Administer budgets, schedules, and performance standards in order to achieve the plans which maximize the company's sales and profits objectives.
- Attend surgeries and ensure top-quality surgeon education on products by assisting in the preparation and running of surgeon training courses which may include didactic and cadaver labs. Participate in VIP tours and assist/ fill in for product managers as required.
- Direct activities between marketing and other functional areas to ensure product line objectives are achieved on a timely basis.

MEDICAL DEVICE MARKETING

	<ul><li>Lead marketing planning activities for assigned product areas with field sales force, sales managers and senior management in order to identify key target, surgeons, and hospitals by specific product.</li><li>Apply Compliance/ Ethics guidelines to management decisions and interactions with surgeon advocates. Ensure product managers are trained and follow guidelines.</li></ul>

CHAPTER 8

Tips and Tricks to Make Life Easier, Plus Some Invaluable Resources

This chapter is the equivalent of the 'catch-all' drawer of the book...anything useful that did not fit elsewhere is here. Thus, there really is not a neat flow or rhyme/ reason for the information contained in Chapter Eight. However, there are ideas, processes, details, and resources that you may find useful on a practical level.

Pesky marketing fundamentals — when 'fluff' is not so 'fluffy'...

PRODUCT POSITIONING AND MESSAGING — WHY BOTHER?

Medical device as a whole has a tendency to ignore what are considered core, essential elements of the product story in every other industry. I am referring to positioning and messaging of course. The purpose of this short section is two –fold: briefly explore why ignoring it has been relatively successful in the past and why ignoring it is not going to carry the day going forward.

First — why has a lack of clear product position and messages not been an issue? Well, for one thing, the fact that no one has done it makes it easier — and in a field where engineering feature/ function/ benefit rule, positioning and messaging have been historically seen as trying to 'dress up' or even 'obscure' the truth rather than just stating facts. Secondly, device marketing requires a high level of technical expertise, even more so than classical marketing background, which can lead to non-marketing people running/ leading the marketing team. The net result is that power of having a consistent message/ position has not been harnessed, most often because the very people who should be driving for it do not fully grasp or understand how to develop it or drive it.

Second – why should you be careful to stay out of this alluring feature/ function/ benefit trap? (It is alluring because of two characteristics: 'everyone is doing it' and it is hard work to develop a precise product position and crisp key messages.) However, taking the significant effort and time to develop positioning and messaging is the best way to create resonance and synergy with the sales team and the internal organization (from the engineers through management) so that the language and image is communicated clearly every time anyone talks about the product. Secondly, the entire marketing campaign, advertising, and promotions will naturally and easily develop out of positioning / messaging if done right. Thus, while discipline and precision are required to create a strong positioning platform, the effort pays off as the campaign and the organization comes together.

Product positioning and messaging – tips

If you have decided to develop a product positioning platform and key messages, there are no shortcuts to make it faster or easier. However, there are a couple of thoughts to consider that may help put you on the right path more quickly...

- One way to consider product positioning is the essence of the product. Instead of trying to come up with something that sounds like it should be printed in calligraphy on white linen paper, remember that this is what you want sales representatives to think and say when they are talking to physicians or even to other sales representatives. If you use big words with long phrases, it is not going to be remembered or used. In fact, if it sounds like your company's mission statement, start over.
- It may help to think about the 'essence of the product' a bit, and to even consider that every product has a personality and probably a few quirks as well. If you are talking to one friend and are telling him/ her about someone that he/she has never met, you usually start out the description or conversation with one to two sentences that are an overview or summary. For instance, you may describe someone as being 'intense with a thoughtful view of the world and somewhat quiet' or perhaps 'the life of the party, always in the middle of things and never met a stranger.' These kind of overview/ summary statements capture the essence of the person's personality, although both of you know critical details are still needed in the conversation to fully appreciate the person. If you can do the same for the product, that's the product positioning platform. It is not comprehensive and more information is naturally required, but you

are attempting to capture the vital and interesting essence of the product that makes it different and unique from other products.
- Last item – if you cannot find anything interesting or unique to say about the product, or if the product 'personality' is simply boring, then there is no chance that the product itself is a blockbuster, and there is not a good chance that the sales team is going to be very interested in it either.

Market segmentation

Market segmentation is another area in which device marketing has certainly not excelled. Fundamentally, it is not a difficult thing to do; in the simplest terms, market segmentation is breaking down possible targets into groups by identifying common characteristics. Healthcare has a tendency to lump groups together by describing physical characteristics or conditions, such as age or geography. However, the most important aspect of segmentation is that the description/ grouping influences behavior or purchasing decisions.

In some cases, easily observable characteristics like residency/ fellowship affiliation may be an accurate predictor of purchasing behavior. However, finding a segmentation strategy that is different or unique may be the critical factor that separates you from your competition. This is especially true if you are in a market with little to differentiate in the way of product. However, a segmentation strategy combined with a strong communication/ messaging program may be a ticket to set your area (company/ product) apart.

To put that into perspective, market segmentation is key to developing a strategy, outlining specific tactics, and determining how to measure for success. By focusing in on one or a few market segments, the product manager can then reasonably put a step-wise plan together on how to attack, from communication to promotion to follow-up. However, without market segmentation, the "marketing campaign" is really just a shotgun blast into the market space with the hope of hitting something. There is less potential for meaningful communication; promotion is a one-time shot and cannot be bundled or built on, and follow-up is virtually non-existent.

In real terms, defining customer groups by past/ current product use, training, or some other category or combination focuses the planning, execution, and metrics of the marketing campaign with a greater likelihood of successful impact.

Marketing campaign metrics

In order to develop metrics for a marketing campaign, you must first determine what success looks like and how you will track it. You also want to know exactly what you want *from* your targets. Are you looking for attention or for action?

As a side note: one of the best ways to both track success/ impact and to gain traction within a campaign is to develop a clear 'call-to-action' within some aspect of the transaction. This can be a one-time event or designed into each step of the campaign. The call-to-action asks the target to do something, perhaps make a call, go to a web site, or send in a response card. Done well, the call-to-action responses give clear indications of whether the campaign is getting heard, and it also can build information on customers (actual or potential) for future use/ conversations as well. (A nice side benefit is the ability to tie response ratio to dollars spent for a nice budget justification/ analysis. What is really nice is being able to use it to gain future budget dollars.)

If you want some guidance on how to define a campaign and objective goals for success, below are some bullet points:

- Establish performance standards – Once the campaign target and objectives have been established, but before the campaign has actually been developed, a SMART goal needs to be established. (SMART standing for the old stand-by specific, measurable, attainable, realistic, and timely.) Even better, align campaign goals with the revenue and profit goals of the company. It not only assists in honing the campaign targeting and timing, but also ensures that the marketing function is a real contributor to the organization.
- Specify data requirements – Data requirements are ideally prospective in nature, something that can be collected as the campaign goes forward. These can also be supplemented with retrospective data analysis.
- Establish data collection systems – In addition to the interim campaign metrics, there has to be systems to collect hard data throughout. If tied to revenue and profit goals, this can be established with the accounting department, although some time beforehand to ensure the necessary reports exist is usually advisable.
- Analyze and monitor marketing activities – As data starts flowing in from the interim collection points (i.e., call-to-action responses) start immediately tracking and assessing effectiveness of the campaign.
- Adjust strategy and tactics – As data becomes available, make changes to the message and to the communication plan. Again, possible changes and timing should have already been considered and triggers for when the changes happen discussed in order to avoid confusion and delay. It is best to approach a campaign by testing messages with target audiences,

especially when the dollar spent is large.

What does 'upstream' versus 'downstream' mean in marketing?

A recent tendency to split the cradle-to-grave marketing model that has traditionally dominated the medical marketing field has surfaced in companies of all sizes and in many device categories. The most common method is to split marketing into an upstream/ strategic/ global part and a downstream/ tactical/ regional part. As with most organizational changes, there are some positive aspects to these changes and some challenges as well. However, on a personal level, these are roles with which you may want to be familiar and completely understand so that you are prepared for success, regardless of whether your organization is considering these changes or if you are interviewing in a company that has this type of structure in place.

DEFINITION OF ROLES

Splitting the product manager role into two parts is a bit problematic because so many activities and functions are tied together in a complex, multi-factorial pattern. Nonetheless a belief has developed in many organizations that forcing greater attention in focal aspects of marketing will drive greater performance, improve efficiency, and ultimately increase sales and profit. While every business must determine for itself what key facets of marketing are worth the extra attention to drive all these improvements, there seems to be a great deal of consistency thus far within medical devices in breaking one product management role into two more concentrated areas. The general agreement seems to be that efforts should be concentrated on setting strategy and speeding product development/ launch process is one core area, while the second spotlight has been generally directed to more fully integrating with local/ regional markets and sales teams in order to improve true market communication and grow share profitably.

Strategic marketing is referred to within many organizations as the *upstream* or *global* function. As the names imply, this aspect of marketing now focuses on the big picture strategy and product launch mapping, gathering/ coordinating global voice-of-customer activities, and working with design teams/ internal processes to get new products out of the pipeline that will grow sales. Their job is to figure out where the new opportunities are going to be and to get the products and support in place in order for the company to capture share/ sales and meet strategic objectives now and in the future. The hallmark of strategic marketing is *thought*. This is not to say 'no action,' just that it is the *how* and *why* part of the equation.

Tactical marketing is often called *downstream* or *regional* and typically involves having marketing teams embedded into key regions/ countries throughout the world. The basic regions usually represented are U.S./ Americas, Europe, Austral-Asia, and Emerging Market, although these can be split many different ways and into much smaller 'bites'. However, the key aspect from a marketing perspective is that each region has its own marketing team that is responsible for the tactical execution on a quarterly/ monthly basis to meet sales/ profit/ product launch targets. These are the people that actually make the plan come to life, figuring out how to fully 'scoop' an opportunity at a local/ regional level. These teams are characterized by *action*, not implying lack of thought necessarily, but more that their mission is around *what* and *when* functions.

One very critical point is that there must be a constant and open flow of communication between these two parts of marketing. In the cradle-to-grave model, a product manager 'owned' the product globally and often still worked with some regional marketing or sales support people for specific projects, but he/ she was still the central repository of information regarding the product. However, with the upstream/ downstream model, this is no longer the case. Information about where the product line is going and future technology resides with the upstream manager, while the downstream managers in each region knows much more about new competitive threats, pricing pressures, and market dynamics. In order for the strategy to be on target – and thus the products/ support delivered to be effective, the information flow between the groups must happen constantly and without impediment.

TRANSITION ZONES

So if upstream marketing handles strategy from a global level and downstream marketing executes local tactics, where do the two meet? The answer is really that they meet all the time, every day – because the global strategy has to feed into marketing plans and market info/ competition has to feed into strategic analysis. However, those are all soft lines and don't get into the heart of this question: where are the turf wars likely to happen?

The answer to *that* question is: at product launch. The line in the sand between upstream and downstream marketing is usually product launch. Upstream marketing works with the engineering/ internal teams and with customers to develop the product, with feedback and input from downstream peers of course. However, the downstream regions are responsible for the actual launch within their regions/ countries. The 'turf wars' over issues of control typically happen during the launch process, with a couple of usual triggers.

- The sales budget — especially if each region doesn't feel ownership on numbers for which they are 'signed up' and/or if the launch is late and sales are in jeopardy.
- When a region/ country does not feel listened to — 'their' physicians are not part of voice-of-customer exercises and they do not feel included in the launch process.
- 'That is not my job' or 'you are not pulling your weight' issues that often arise when there is a transition to this upstream/ downstream format.

Ultimately, getting into a blame game is a short-term win at best, and usually ends up in an all-out war somewhere down the road. Additionally, the issues above result from lack of communication and collaboration — and from feeling the need to take control of an 'out-of-control' situation. Getting marketing teams to work together is similar to the old adage about herding cats. Just like herding cats, the best way to move forward is to be open and clear with your communication and your efforts to collaborate and be careful not to appear like you are trying to control others. It is possible — just not easy.

To help in understanding the differences in roles, and the areas most likely to cause contention, a chart is below with a list of marketing activities that are divided up into what is commonly considered 'upstream' versus 'downstream' responsibilities. The darker gray boxes indicate launch transition zones or hand-off points where the two areas must truly work as one in order to effectively and efficiently accomplish the launch. The lighter gray boxes indicate areas in which conflicts are also likely to arise and the need to collaborate can easily turn into a battle for control.

One example of this is in building financials for product launch, including sales projections, ASP's, and ramp time to first sale. Since this is often owned by upstream marketing, yet left to downstream marketing to execute, the potential for conflict and resentment is tremendous.

◄ MEDICAL DEVICE MARKETING

Marketing Activity	Upstream/ Strategic	Overlap	Downstream/ Tactical
Strategic planning	Responsible		Provide input
Environment/market intel	Responsible		Provide input on local/ reg'l info
Competitive intel	Responsible at global level	Communication & coordination required	Responsible at local/ reg'l level
Technology assessment	Responsible		Provide input
Global acquistions	Responsible		Provide input as requested
Local/ reg'l acquisitions	Provide input as requested		Responsible
Licensing agreements	Responsible at global level		Responsible at local/ reg'l level
Financials - new project	Responsible	Heavy communication req'd	Provide input
Financials - existing product	(Co-responsible in some orgs)	Heavy communication req'd	Responsible
VOC - new product idea	Responsible	Coordination ensures good customer input & intel	Provide input & expertise
VOC - assess market/ technology	Responsible	Same as above	Provide input & expertise
VOC - assess design concept(s)	Responsible	Same as above	Provide input & expertise
VOC - input on core product position	Responsible	Careful review for strong global message & appeal	Provide input, review
VOC - launch evaluations	Secondarily responsible	Shared - usually transition point in launch	Primarily responsible
VOC - launch advertising/ messaging	Provide input	Some orgs require Upstream approval of core message pieces	Responsible
VOC - input on existing products	Provide input as requested		Responsible
Forecast - new product	Responsible	Detailed coordination req'd	Provide input
Forecast- existing product	Input is org dependent	Some org's's use upstream to collate & review	Responsible
Inventory/ backorder - launch	Responsible	Communication & coordination required	Provide input on prioritization
Inventory/ backorder - exist product	Input/ assist is org dependent	Org dependent - most keep w/ downstream	Usually responsible
Training - launches	Responsible for technical content & product positioning	Transition point of launch	Responsible for rep/ surgeon training plan & execution
Training - existing products	Provide input as requested	Upstream may step in if product re-positioned/ re-launched	Responsible
Sales support/ literature - launch	Responsible for transfer of core technical content & positioning	Transition point of launch	Responsible for tactical launch plan & execution
Sales support/ literature - exist prod.	Provide input as requested		Responsible
Customer/ physician requests & calls	Provide assist as requested		Responsible
Sales team requests & calls	Provide assist as requested		Responsible
Setting price	Responsible	Communication on global impact required	Provide input
Discount policy	Input is org dependent	Some orgs require Upstream approval of discount plan	Responsible

Resources for gathering data, and generally helpful info

SECONDARY DATA SOURCE LIST

The information below is intended as reference, not as light reading material. As you are looking for research reports or market analysis, the following sources may help you. However, please note that these are not free – you/ your company will have to purchase reports, buy subscriptions/ memberships, or in some cases become involved with the brokerage firms in order to have full access to their analysis/ research reports. This is simply intended as a guide to get you started; in no way is it comprehensive, since more sources get added every day.

Frost and Sullivan
http://www.frost.com/prod/servlet/svcg.pag/HCMD
1.877.463.7678

Frost and Sullivan's Medical Devices Research and Consulting practice provides global industry analysis, custom consulting, growth consulting (strategy consulting), and market research and forecasts that are designed to help your business grow.

DataMonitor
www.datamonitor.com
Medical devices research store index:
http://www.datamonitor.com/store/Browse/?Ntt=medical+device&N=4294854036

The Datamonitor Group aims to help its clients operating in the pharmaceuticals, healthcare and biotechnology fields, offering world-leading products and services to meet the challenges of this rapidly evolving marketplace. MedTRACK is a fully integrated, global biomedical database providing the most comprehensive one-stop-shop for information on companies, products, deals, venture financing, and epidemiology.

---

iData Research Inc
www.idataresearch.net
Tel (604)266-6933

iData Research is an incorporated international market research and consulting group focused on providing market intelligence, monitoring and competitive insight for the medical device and pharmaceutical companies around the world.

Millennium Research Group, Inc.
www.mrg.net
T: (416) 364-7776

Focused on the medical technology industry, MRG provides its clients with the benefits of its specialized market expertise through syndicated reports, ongoing Marketrack™ projects, and customized consulting solutions.

MEDICAL DEVICE MARKETING

Global Markets Direct:
www.globalmarketsdirect.com
Report Store
www.globalmarketsdirect.com/CategorySearchResult.aspx?Title=Medical_Devices

The Global Markets Direct Report Store features thousands of high quality company and market research reports across a broad range of industries. Browse or search their collection of reports today to access the latest in business intelligence from some of the world's leading publishers.

Medtech Insight (division of Windhover Information, Inc.)
www.medtechinsight.com
Tel (949)219-0150

Medtech Insight provides business information and intelligence on new trends, technologies, and companies in the medical device, diagnostics, and biotech marketplace. They offer a broad range of products and services for medical technology executives

---

Knowledge Enterprises
www.theorthopeople.com
Tel (440)247-9051

Founded in 1992, ORTHOWORLD is the only publisher in the world focused solely on the global orthopaedic market. Their singular mission is helping orthopaedic companies and individuals achieve their growth directives. They strive to help their members and subscribers stay abreast of industry developments by providing timely, strategically managed news and insights relating to developments, trends and technologies in virtually every product segment within the musculoskeletal sector—including reconstructive, trauma, spine, arthroscopy, sports medicine, biologics and more.

Orthopaedics This Week
www.ryortho.com
1-877-817-6450

Publishes *Orthopaedics This Week*, part of RRY publications.

Leerink Swann and Company – Health Care Equity Research
www.leerink.com
(888) 347-2342

Leerink Swann is committed to bring the most knowledgeable healthcare investment bank. They are an industry specialist firm, focused exclusively on healthcare.

Bear, Stearns and Co. Inc.
www.bearstearns.com
JP Morgan company research -- https://mm.jpmorgan.com/disclosures/company/
(212) 272-2000

J.P. Morgan Securities Investment Professionals are among the most experienced and creative in the industry and excel at leveraging the vast resources of one of the world's leading global financial institutions on behalf of their clients. (As part of our integration with J.P. Morgan, we have changed our name to *J.P. Morgan Securities*.)

Canaccord Adams Research,
www.canaccordadams.com
Database/ research searchable by stock name - www.canaccordadams.com/research/Disclosure.htm

---

PearlDiver
www.pearldiverinc.com

PearlDiver is building the orthopedic industry's largest online repository of data and information. PearlDiver is an emerging growth company leader in the life sciences information industry. Its services include search and analysis software and database technologies, consulting services and information based strategic advisory services.

Books from the FDA

The FDA provides a list of books, pamphlets, and other resources available at a price to the medical device community. The resources range widely in content but can be useful and are clear indicators of FDA and government perspective and interest. They can be found at FDA Pharmaceutical and Medical Device Books http://www.fdanews.com/store/section/books?index=7

One book title worth highlighting is *Device off label promotion: case studies to prepare for increased enforcement* as the FDA continues to define regulatory nuance, and even more so in light of the criminal indictments currently pending against several corporations and marketing executives because of alleged off-label promotion.

If you are unfamiliar with the current situation facing Synthes, Norian, and Stryker executives because of charges by the FDA of off-label marketing, you may want to check out the articles listed below and do some additional research since these will be dated by the time you read them. Understanding what constitutes off-label marketing as well as the risk/ penalties will help you assess and avoid potential problems, which could include both criminal and civil lawsuits. While you may or may not be a prime target for an investigation as a product manager, you certainly will want to be aware and ensure that you make wise decisions for both yourself and your company.

Online articles regarding off-label marketing and charges:

> Synthes, Norian, and four executives charged in connection with unlawful clinical trials. (June 2009). Medical Devices Business Review. Retrieved Jan 2, 2010 at http://www.medicaldevices-business-review.com/news/synthes_norian_and_four_executives_charged_in_connection_with_unlawful_clinical_trials_090616/.
>
> Synthes indicted over Norian XR bone cement tests. (June, 2009). NewsInferno.com. Retrieved Jan. 2, 2010 at http://www.newsinferno.com/archives/6982.
>
> Medical device company indicted for off-label marketing and statements made to FDA during regulatory inquiry. (June 2009). Foley and Lardner LLP. Retrieved Jan 2, 2010 at http://www.foley.com/publications/pub_detail.aspx?pubid=6123.
>
> MassDevice Staff. (Oct. 2009). Details emerge in federal case against Stryker Biotech. Mass Device. Retrieved Jan. 2, 2010 at http://www.massdevice.com/news/details-emerge-federal-case-against-stryker-biotech.

PUBLICATIONS FOR MEDICAL DEVICE BUSINESS PROFESSIONALS

While medical device consulting and advertising firms are plentiful, having the dollars and the time to spend getting input for each and every project is improbable and unrealistic. Rather, gaining the confidence and the skills to develop and implement plans – and to sell your plans to internals teams and company executives – is a critical aspect of career growth. Thus, it is a good idea to develop a network of device marketers with whom you can share ideas and it is also nice to have some sources of new ideas to consider and incorporate as the opportunity comes along.

One possible source of information and ideas is the publications that are targeted to medical device marketers. These magazines can come in a variety of formats with different types of content. Some are more formal and published less often, while others are oriented toward the web and weekly publication. They also range from newspaper-style reporting to more journalistic, HBR-type of content. Regardless, it is helpful to have a range and variety of sources that you can use routinely, with a few to which you can look when something more or different would be helpful. Below is a list of a handful of publications that have a strong history within medical devices, plus offer additional services that can help in some way. By no means is this an exhaustive list; there are numerous other publications that are available, with more added all the time.

- <u>The Healthcare Sales and Marketing Network</u> – published since 1998, the magazine reviews device news, up to ten personalized tracking reports, search capabilities of archives, and online bio information for networking for $35 per year. http://salesandmarketingnetwork.com/.

- <u>Journal of Medical Marketing</u> – published quarterly in print and online format, although you can get table of contents and purchase articles as requested online without a subscription. Content is more academic in nature and quite thorough versus the magazine-style format of the Healthcare Network (above). Cost is $275 online only and $290 online and print in the U.S. for a <u>personal</u> subscription. (NOTE: They also have a Journal for Targeting, Measurement, and Analysis for Marketing available through the same publisher which may be helpful in developing marketing campaign metrics and budgeting.) http://www.palgrave-journals.com/jmm/index.html.

- <u>Medical Marketing and Media</u> – published monthly, MM&M has covered pharma and device since 2006 and offers whitepapers and other services in addition to the newsletter. Subscriptions run $148 for one year and $250 for two years. They are also known for their yearly career and salary survey data specific to the medical device field, which is priced separately at $295. http://www.mmm-online.com/.

INDUSTRY ASSOCIATIONS

While not traditionally considered a resource, there are at least two device industry associations of which are worth being aware. The first organization,

AdvaMed, is definitely a source of information for most companies with their Code of Ethics for Health Care Providers. While non-members do not have to sign on, many voluntarily choose to comply and AdvaMed has a section of their website dedicated to training materials for non-members. There may be other industry associations as well, but these are two of which to be aware and consider accessing if you are with either a large or small organization.

- AdvaMed (Advanced Medical Technology Association) – The AdvaMed organization is an advocacy group and has offices in DC, although it is a much larger cooperative with global intent and touches on legal, regulatory, reimbursement, and economic initiatives. AdvaMed members sign the Code of Ethics that govern interactions with HealthCare Providers (HCP's), although many non-member companies also comply with these rules as well. *These guidelines are mainly targeted at marketing and sales activities* and should be familiar. The website offers training information for both members and non-members on the guidelines. The AdvaMed website is listed for reference, both for the guidelines and to use for other resource material as well. Additionally, an article published about the guidelines is also included to provide perspective on how these rules are seen by the legislative bodies and the media in general. http://www.advamed.org/MemberPortal/.

Perrone, M. (March, 2009). Medical device industry rolls out marketing guidelines: Manufacturing.net. Found on Jan. 2, 2010 at http://www.manufacturing.net/News-Medical-Device-Industry-Rolls-Out-Marketing-Guidelines-030509.aspx?menuid=762.

- MDMA (Medical Device Manufacturers Association) – MDMA is an organization for small device companies with under $5M in annual sales and has been in place since 1992. It is an advocacy voice in DC on behalf of device firms, as well as a source of information and guidance that can be especially helpful for smaller firms that lack some of the resources/public voice of the larger companies. There are annual dues. More information can be found at http://www.medicaldevices.org/public/.

Conclusion

The medical device industry is a unique field that involves working with experts to figure out how to repair or replace parts of the human body, letting people work and function better. Working in this industry is rewarding because you know that it really benefits someone – patient, surgeon, O.R. team, etc. That knowledge is what makes all of us work harder and feel good at the end of the day.

Why do I believe that marketing is so fundamental to successful medical device companies? Because marketing makes sure that the full continuum of customers are heard, that the sales team understands the fundamentals of the product, and generally connects all the separate pieces together by communicating within the company. The marketing team spans strategy to encompass tactical execution and stretches across every part of the organization, touching on each aspect of the device in the process.

Marketing medical devices continues to be a career that is challenging and personally and professionally satisfying. At the end of a hard day, week, or month, contributing something that is a tangible benefit makes it worthwhile. Medical device marketing can give you that sense of accomplishment.

CPSIA information can be obtained
at www.ICGtesting.com
Printed in the USA
BVHW08s0735190818
524959BV00005B/197/P

9 781432 750725